ERIC SYKES'
COMEDY
HEROES

ERIC SYKES' COMEDY HEROES

This edition first published in 2006 by
Virgin Books Ltd
Thames Wharf Studios
Rainville Road
London
W6 9HA

First published in the UK in 2003 by Virgin Books Ltd

ISBN-10 07535 1188 6
ISBN-13 978 0 7535 1188 6

Typeset by Virgin Books.
Printed and bound in Great Britain by Bookmarque Ltd.

All pictures come from the author's private collection.

CONTENTS

INTRODUCTION

My Comedy Heroes all have one thing in common . . . they all make me laugh and by this I mean a healthy, warm explosion of mirth, a belly laugh which has little to do with the whooo hooo, hands clapping above the head of today's audiences reminding the comedian that they are part of the show as well and, furthermore, they've paid their entrance fee for the privilege.

Naturally, not all my Heroes in this book will be everybody's cup of tea, God help us if they were . . . we would really be on the slippery slopes to global hopelessness. Humour comes in all shapes and sizes and is freely available, but this does not mean that everyone is a humorist. Most pubs in this country boast their own comedian: a person who rattles off the latest jokes, and offices, factories and shops each possess their own styles of comedian. The same jokes are available to all, but it is the professional comedian who takes his life in his hands every night in front of different audiences from pubs, offices, factories and shops, providing new material for the local joke tellers.

Now that this book is finished, several more comedians I would have liked to include have just occurred to me. I'm sure this applies to most of us . . . having just made a speech, the best lines then spring to mind.

One of my earliest mates of the late forties, Max Bygraves, whose friendship I still enjoy today, is not included in this book because primarily he is not a comedian, he is one of our best-known entertainers and, like a one-legged man, he does not qualify for the marathon. Bruce Forsyth, dancer/pianist/king of the game-show hosts, falls into the same category; had I been asked to write a book entitled Heroes of Entertainment they would certainly have featured.

However, I am sure that my choices in this book would make a most wonderful Royal Command Performance . . . in fact between them they've probably done about fifty as it is. What is more important, most of my Comedy Heroes who have passed on still had a list of engagements in the diary when the grim reaper closed the Box Office.

Professional comedians are but a minute handful of happiness and it is to those dedicated few I raise my hat.

NORMAN COLLIER

Goo…click…vening…click click…very body – a microphone breakdown

PROFILE

Born: 25 December 1925

Place of birth: Hull, Yorkshire

Norman's first professional engagement was a summer season with Cliff Richard and the Shadows in 1963. He continued to work mainly in pubs and clubs until becoming an 'overnight success' at the 1971 Royal Variety Performance where his act earned him a standing ovation.

Selected theatre: *Make 'Em Laugh* (2002)

Selected TV: *Des O' Connor Tonight, Parkinson, Live From Her Majesty's, The Main Attraction* (1984), *Mr H Is Late* (1998)

There are not many people outside this book who have reduced me to helpless laughter but in my opinion Norman Collier is two furlongs ahead of the field. From the very first time I caught him on television I was a devotee and I didn't even know his name.

He was so refreshingly different from the 'unclip the mike – "There was this Irishman" ' brigade of comedians. Norman simply came on stage and was a cockerel. In real life a cockerel struts amongst his harem in the farmyard and to watch his arrogant steps, head jerking all over the place, eyes popping with an expression of affronted dignity, a cockerel has to be the comedian of the animal kingdom. When Norman Collier walked on stage, using his jacket as wings, clucking his way to the front, you'd be forgiven for thinking that real live cockerels were taking the Mickey.

One year I was in a comedy play in Blackpool star-ring Les Dawson. Just along the road Russ Abbott was appearing and at another theatre was the inimi-table Norman Collier. During the summer season, as is customary, we met for a jolly in a tearoom adjacent. Les told a few jokes, Russ added a few of his own, and I put in my four pence, and then came the pièce de résist-ance – Norman Collier. Sitting at the table using the salt cellar, cutlery, table lamp and table cloth, even table legs, each item became something else in his hands – a micro-scope, a lady trying on a hat. It is impossible to do justice in words to this manic, wordless, excruciating fifteen minutes of sheer inspiration. The waitress, the owner of the cafe and faces peering through the window were all Norman needed to inspire him to a higher plane of quality comic invention. Even dear old Les had to wipe the tears from his eyes and I've only seen him in that condition once before when it was his turn to buy a round.

Looking into Norman's tired, faded blue eyes, one has the uncanny feeling that he has been here before. His inventions and humorous imaginations could be centuries old. It is not too incredible to believe he once called Shakespeare 'Willie'; for all we know he might have been 'the bard' himself. But these are only my flights of fancy. Norman is unfathomable. Paradoxically, his talents are against him inasmuch as he would not be content with an act no matter how brilliant, its very repetitiveness every performance would be anathema to him.

Norman is held in high esteem by his fellow professionals, who appreciate his mercurial mind which lifts him to heights of comedy invention. However, this is not the case with a large section of the public. The reason for this is simple – unlike *Coronation Street* or *The Bill*, Norman is not known on television. It is a sad indictment of our age when he is not as well known as the weatherman or any of *The Archers*, and if you're not on television some people think of you as retired, or better still, dead.

When I spoke to Norman on the telephone he recounted some of his experiences in his turbulent career. He wasn't bitter or despondent; on the contrary he was laughing his head off as if all these events he was telling me about happened to somebody else.

On one occasion, he was leaving the stage door and as he did so a little urchin stepped forward and said in a Brummy accent, 'Hey mister, are you in the show?' to which Norman replied, 'Yes.'

'Can I have your autograph?' Norman, being the gentleman he is, said, 'Of course,' and held out his hand for an autograph book.

The boy didn't move and after a moment or two looked up at Norman and said, 'Have you got a piece of paper?'

Norman fiddled about in his pocket and found an old theatre bill.

'Will that do?' he said.

The lad said, 'Yes, have you got a pencil?' Again Norman found a pencil, scribbled his name on the bill and handed it over.

The lad scrutinised it closely then he said, 'Have you got a rubber?' Norman spluttered with high glee as he told me this and before I could ask the name of the theatre he was on to his next episode.

Apparently, an elderly woman shuffled up and stopped him in the street. 'Hang on a minute,' she said. 'Aren't you Norman Conquest?' Norman said he wasn't and as he moved off she shouted to his back, 'Well you look like him!'

Poor old Norman, he doesn't half pick them. A couple of years ago, arriving in Blackpool to begin a summer season, he drove into the car park at the back of the hotel. As he got out the car park attendant approached, beaming and said, 'I know you.'

Norman gave him the obligatory smile and started to offload his props from the boot of the car. 'Go on,' said the attendant. 'Get it out.'

'Get what out?' said Norman.

'You know,' smiled the man. Norman shook his head and turned to lift another piece of equipment from the boot when the man repeated, 'Go on, get it out.'

Exasperated, Norman said, 'Get what out?'

Delighted the man said, 'The Emu.'

Unfortunately, Norman attracts nuts like a hungry squirrel. It is one of the hazards of our business. Norman is used to this encroachment of his civil liberties and deftly lobs the ball over the net, a remarkable feat as he doesn't play tennis.

But Norman Collier will be remembered for various comedy appearances on stage, mainly as an announcer talking into a defective microphone or the man winding down a car window to argue with another driver.

My admiration for Norman Collier is immense for many things, amongst these his lack of desire to jump on the stairway to 'the big time', preferring to keep his feet on the ground, wondering at and enjoying his ability to see the funny side in order to share his humour with anybody who can spare the time to stop and appreciate. You'll do for me, Norman.

PETER COOK AND DUDLEY MOORE

University degrees are not always a bad thing

PROFILE

Peter Cook
Born: 17 November 1937
Place of birth: Torquay, Devon

Dudley Moore
Born: 19 April 1935
Place of birth: Dagenham, Essex

Peter studied modern languages at Cambridge where he auditioned successfully for Footlights. He was then commissioned to write *Pieces of Eight*, a West End revue for Kenneth Williams. The son of a railway worker, Dudley overcame the handicap of a club foot to win a music scholarship to Oxford.

He teamed up with Peter Cook, Alan Bennett and Jonathan Miller in the hit revue *Beyond the Fringe.*

Selected theatre: (Cook and Moore) *The Wrong Box* (1966), *Bedazzled* (1968), *Monte Carlo or Bust* (1969), *The Bed Sitting Room* (1969), *The Hound of the Baskervilles* (1977); (Cook) *The Rise and Rise of Michael Rimmer* (1979), *Yellowbeard* (1983), *Without a Clue* (1988); (Moore) *Foul Play* (1978), *10* (1979), *Wholly Moses* (1980), *Arthur* (1981), *Six Weeks* (1982), *Lovesick* (1983), *Romantic Comedy* (1983)

Selected TV: (Cook and Moore) *Not Only...But Also* (1965-70), *Goodbye Again* (1968-69); (Cook) *On the Braden Beat* (1964), *Alice in Wonderland* (1966), *Peter Cook and Co.* (1980), *The Two of Us* (1981-82), *A Life in Pieces* (1990-1991), *The Clive Anderson Show* (1993)

Peter Cook died: 9 January 1995

Dudley Moore died: 27 March 2002

I've always been slightly wary of students spending four or five years in the cloistered walls of universities, protected from the harsh reality of the outside world, learning to be doctors, lawyers, teachers, etc., then graduating with honours only to decide to take up a career in comedy.

Being a Lancashire lad I believed that comedy was born out of poverty, hardship, poor housing; in fact, humour in the old days was a necessity – laughter was free. So you will understand my antipathy towards fully qualified doctors, lawyers, teachers, et al, having the temerity to invade our world of comedy. However, that was my bigoted view until, in the early sixties, Peter Cook, Dudley Moore, Alan Bennett and Jonathan Miller, all from universities, exploded on to the West End Stage like a scud missile, lighting up theatreland in a show called *Beyond the Fringe*. The theatre was jam-packed, which is always a good sign, and the second most important ingredient was they were laughing fit to bust. Even more surprising, so was I, because it wasn't my kind of humour – it was beyond that. Nor was it born out of poverty, hunger and poor housing; it was comedy that transcended the earthiness of parochial humour. Witty, intelligent, above all hilarious, as if someone had opened the curtains to admit a shaft of bright sunlight, it was the beginning of a new branch on the comedy tree and it introduced Peter Cook and Dudley Moore.

Peter, whose wit was as sharp and sparkling as a cut-throat razor, and his portrayal of his no-hoper character 'E.L. Wisty' was unforgettable. I will never forget Peter on his haunches, flat cap, untidy mac, intoning in a doleful, earnest voice the unfairness of life condemning him to work underground as a coal-miner when his burning desire was to be a brain surgeon. Although burning is too positive a word to describe the boring old codger 'E.L. Wisty', he droned on remorselessly that there was little or no stimulating conversation down a mine. 'Oh, look, here's a lump of coal' or 'Is that my pick axe, Jack?' are hardly topics for an intelligent debate, whereas one would meet a better class of people amongst the brain surgeon fraternity.

Even now I smile with sweet nostalgia at the recollec-tion. On the other hand, little Dudley Moore came from a working-class background but struggled to eminence, being an organ scholar at Oxford, graduating with honours. How's that for a little tearaway from Dagenham, East London? I shouldn't think that Dagenham was awash with organs, so Dudley's achievements were all the more remarkable. I mean, what possessed him to take it up in the first place, an enormous hulk of a thing that's hardly the instrument to take on tour? A loud, noisy contraption suitable only for 'The Wedding March' and a couple of light pieces by Bach but certainly not 'Oh I Do Like To Be Beside The Seaside' , as bellowed out of the Tower Ball-room, Blackpool.

But then sit Dudley at the piano and there was the cherry on the cake. I could listen and watch his fingers slide around the keyboard until 'Time, Gentlemen Please'. It was magic and Dudley must have found it a merciful relief from the 'Mighty Wurlitzer'. There were no stops to pull out and push in and on the piano he had only two pedals for his feet, so he didn't have to dance about frantically as if he had a mouse in his trouser pocket.

But that said, this is not a book about my Musical Heroes, otherwise I would be eulogising about John Williams or Buddy Rich, so back to Pete and Dud in my Hall of Fame. They were well established by the time *Not Only, But Also* hit our television screens, the likes of which I doubt will ever be bettered. To see the two of them in dirty macs, cloth caps and scarves sitting in a pub, side by side, each reminiscing into their pints of beer:

PETE: I had a funny dream last night, Dud. I dreamt there was a tapping on the window, I woke up with a start, it was Sophia Loren. Get away, Sophia, I shouted. I need to get some sleep and I can't when you keep pestering me.

DUD: I had a funny dream, too, Pete . . .

Dud's dream was almost identical, only the lady pestering was different. I have tried to convey this dialogue because it was only later that I discovered that these pub sketches, as with much of their half-hour, were unscripted – an amazing feat in the black and white days of a weekly series. Obviously, they chatted together beforehand as to the subject matter but what a piece of mental gymnastics by these two. Disastrously, most of their output has been wiped, on the order of a Head of Light Entertainment, who probably never watched the show anyway.

I appeared as a guest on one of their *Not Only* shows. As I was an avid fan, I refused firstly on the grounds that I enjoyed the shows so much I couldn't possibly contribute anything that might enhance the show. I also mentioned that if I was in the show I wouldn't be able to watch it, as they were 'live'.

Finally, after much battering, I agreed to do it thinking I'd have a week to prepare my input. I wasn't aware that most of their shows were ad lib until the following morning when the producer rang me up and asked where I was.

I said, 'What's the panic?'

He said, 'The show is tonight.'

'Tonight!' I thought. 'Good grief.' All I knew was that I was in a sketch about 'The Monster from the Deep' but there was no such thing as a script and the show was live. In this sketch Peter was the film director, Dudley the scaly monster from the lagoon and I was the leading man. Peter, discussing the plot, interrupted by Dud, complete in costume with the huge fearsome head under his arm, asking inane questions like, 'When I surface do you want me to roar?' Pete replying they would dub the 'roars' and would be auditioning the 'roarers' tomorrow. All through the dialogue exchanges they kept looking to me to add my oar but I was too far gone. I'd never heard their chatter before and I'm afraid all I could do was laugh. In fact, the more I laughed so did the audience and eventually so did Pete and Dud and that's where we ran out of time. Is it any wonder they're two of my Heroes?

Sadly, they are no longer with us. Several others in this book have also moved on but at least in their cases old age had a lot to do with it. With regards to Peter Cook and Dudley Moore they went well before their allotted three score years and ten. Peter, I suspect, went in a fog of frustration, Dudley in dark depression, but I blame this on his close proximity to the organ during his formative years.

TOMMY COOPER

Funniest man in the world

PROFILE

Born: 9 March 1922

Place of birth: Caerphilly, South Wales

Tommy served in the Horse Guards during WWII and was wounded in action after which he began entertaining the troops. He'd first tried magic tricks when he was given a magic set at the age of eight. In Egypt, during the war, his magic act acquired his trademark fez which he borrowed from a waiter during his act. It got such a laugh, he kept it.

Selected films: *And the Same to You* (1960), *The Cool Mikado* (1963), *The Plank* (1967)

Selected TV: *The Leslie Henson Christmas Eve Party, It's Magic, Cooper's Capers, Cooperama, Life with Cooper, Cooper's Half Hour, The Ed Sullivan Show, The Tommy Cooper Hour*

Died: 15 April 1984.

My favourite watering hole in the late forties was a pub in Kingley Street, a brisk walk from the Palladium stage door, less if you're thirsty. On one occasion, swapping wartime yarns with the Canadian barman, I was explaining how we'd landed on the wrong beach at Normandy when I became aware of a tall, lugubrious man in a long black overcoat at my elbow. The pub was half empty and there was lots of space for him to stand somewhere else. Perhaps he was lonely and possibly a war historian interested in our discussion, or more likely he was just a harassed undertaker worried that people were living longer.

'I'm Tommy Cooper,' he said and at the time I thought it was an odd name for an undertaker. 'I know who you are,' he went on. 'You do Frankie Howerd's scripts,' and in the same breath he said, 'Can I buy you a drink?'

'I'm OK,' I said. 'No, thanks.'

He relaxed immediately and it was only many years later, when we were close mates, I appreciated the enormous compliment he paid me when he uttered those words in the pub – because I could never recall him putting his hand in his pocket to buy a round. On other matters he was a most generous man, he just seemed to have a phobia about buying drinks. That reminds me of one occasion, true incidentally, when Tom stepped out of a taxi he paid the cabbie the exact fare then stuffed something crinkly into his top pocket.

'Have a drink on me,' he said.

'God Bless you, Tom,' shouted the delighted cabbie as he drove off, hoping it was a fiver or, praise the Lord, a tenner. He felt in his pocket and pulled out a teabag!

That was Tom, and such was his popularity it wouldn't surprise me if that teabag, in a glass case, is now on the cabbie's mantelpiece.

But getting back to the pub in Kingley Street . . . by the time we'd left, we were best mates, full of bonhomie and Glenmorangie. I knew now he was a conjurer and he was appearing that night at a club called The Bag of Nails. I offered to carry his suitcase which he told me was full of his props.

It was enormous and so heavy I couldn't help thinking it must be a long act. Thankfully, The Bag of Nails was only down the street. I remember clearly the black door and for a moment I thought he lived there – it couldn't possibly be a nightclub. Tommy knocked in a strange way and a panel in the door slid open and a face appeared. The panel snapped shut and the door opened. Tommy took his suitcase and went in. I remember wondering if I'd ever see him again or, for that matter, if anybody would ever see him again.

In fact, quite a few years went by before I met Tommy for the second time which was in Leicester Square and after our 'Hellos' I said, 'How did it go?'

Straightaway he laughed, 'Oh, The Bag of Nails?' He knew immediately what I was talking about, the bad things never leave you. You ask a one-legged man about his missing member and he'll tell you in a flash the date, the time and how the surgeons had made a mistake and that another patient with a bad leg had his tonsils out. And so it was with Tommy. He described to me his first and last disastrous appearance at The Bag of Nails. Apparently, the clientele of that club wasn't exactly from Who's Who, but there'd be plenty about them in police records. Mainly Tommy's audience that night were villains, hardmen and hoodlums out on a night's bender.

Tom, smart in dinner jacket, was a target. Some of the lads, well-laced with sherbet, were trying to knock Tom's fez off with bread rolls – even their women joined in. At the time, Tommy was doing his glass, bottle, bottle, glass routine. The stage now looked as if the bakery had taken a direct hit and Tommy's patience snapped.

'Stop that!' he shouted at a man, scarred white face brought on by years inside, red-nosed in celebration of his release. It was a bad choice. When Tom said 'Stop that' the whole place went silent and Tom said he was petrified. He knew he'd end up in concrete and half hoped it would be in one of the supports propping up the M4. When I asked why, he said, 'So I could keep an eye on my house.'

I asked what did happen, and apparently the bloke said, 'Why shouldn't I throw bread rolls at your fez?'

In a panic Tom replied, 'Because I haven't got an ad-lib for people throwing bread rolls at my hat.'

There was a moment's pause then the whole audience laughed and he was able to continue his act, but had he made the wrong reply we may never have known the funniest man in the world.

In every prospective comedian's career there is a 'Bag of Nails', perhaps more than one and if, like Tommy Cooper, you can put these hazards behind you, the next one can be easier to handle. Eventually, with luck, you're at the top and, having survived these experiences, you'll stay there.

Tom and I had many good times together and a million laughs. One of the highlights was *The Plank*. A silent film, Tom playing an inept builder having lost a plank of wood wandering all round East Acton looking for it. As director my only difficulty with Tom was getting him not to act funny but to be himself – what a paradox! For instance, in one scene he just had to walk about 50 yards down a street towards the camera looking for 'the plank' and before the 'action' I said to the cameraman, 'Don't turn over on this one.' Guessing how Tom was going to come down the street, I wasn't about to shoot useless film.

'Action, Tommy,' I shouted and down the street he came. It was funny, but it wasn't real.

'OK,' I said, 'we'll just take another one for insurance.' Then I took Tom gently on one side.

'This time just walk normally,' I said.

'I was acting,' he protested.

'Listen, Tom,' I said. 'If I'd wanted an actor I'd have got one, as it is I've got the funniest man in the world. Just walk naturally and normally down the street looking for the plank.'

On his second take he came down the street naturally, as himself, but he was unconvinced; he didn't think he was funny. It was only when the filming was over and I was dubbing the music that I put the finishing touches to Tommy's walk down the street. The drummer placed his snare drum in front of the screen and drummed a march to Tom's feet. It was perfect, even the musicians laughed.

When the film was finally put to bed it was shown to a selected audience and, naturally, Tom was present. He was laughing along with the audience but he was perturbed when the next scene would show him walking down the street. However, he need not have worried. It was hilarious, thanks largely to the drummer's accompaniment to his footsteps. Tom's walk took on the semblance of a carefully choreographed piece of footwork. The audience loved it and Tom, a happy boy now, said, 'Ah, but you never told me you were going to put music to it.'

I quote this example because it applies to many of my Comedy Heroes – they cannot accept that they are funny people. Tom was always well turned out in very expensive suits, collar and tie, hair immaculate. It doesn't matter how well tailored the clothes are, if the body inside is out of sync there's no chance. Tommy had a very long body, and legs better suited to a smaller man, but to compensate, his feet were large and set permanently at ten minutes to two in order to take his weight. Poor Tom was badly served at the body shop. When he walked into a room he imagined himself as 007 or Michael Caine, but people would begin to smile or laugh out loud. Granted, this reaction was generated by his stage popularity but it is hard to tell a six foot, ex-trooper that, however smart his suit is or how shiny his shoes, he will always be a man of comedy.

Rather than persist in calling Tom a funny man I much prefer to call him a man of fun with his 'Have a drink on me' in the cabbie's top pocket. It was harmless. I never heard him taking a rise out of anybody or making fun of someone unable to fight back; mainly, he turned the laugh on himself.

For instance, Tom and I were doing an hour's show together on television and had agreed to meet in the pub next to the studio at twelve o'clock sharp, at which time the pub would still be empty, and Tom and I and the producer, Denis Kirkland, would discuss the show. Denis and I arrived just before twelve. I was pleased with the script and hoped Tom would enjoy it as well. We were going to discuss the casting, giving us three weeks before the first rehearsal.

As it turned out, midday came and went but no Tommy. One or two more customers sauntered in and it was now nearly half past and by this time I was rapidly getting to the boil. Quarter to one and by now the pub was full but still no Tom. Our table was directly facing the door in a position to spot all who entered and Tom was definitely not one of them. With the pub now crowded, our meeting would be a non-starter. With the hubbub it would be impossible to shout our ideas at each other.

It was after one o'clock when the door opened and Tom stood there. For a moment, the noise dwindled and the customers stared in amazement at the apparition at the door. Tom was standing there in pyjamas, slippers and a bowler hat. Then he made his way to the table as if posing for a portrait of 'When did you last see your father?'

Removing his bowler, he said, 'I'm sorry, I couldn't get up.' The pub was in uproar and I, five minutes ago ready to let fly, was now helpless with laughter. Situation normal.

On another occasion, when we were making *The Plank*, Tom and I were having lunch in a nearby pub. All the others who were filming that day came with us, most of the cast instantly recognisable being well-known in films, television or stage or in the case of Henry Cooper, the boxing ring, James Hunt, Formula One or whatever . . . We were given a long table in an upstairs room, that is all except Tom and me. We were still dressed in the scruffy overalls we wore in the film, and the barman barred our way when we were about to go upstairs. It was obvious he wasn't English, he just knew enough of our language to stop us going upstairs.

'Private party,' he said. 'Very important people.'

He was trying to usher us towards the public bar when Henry Cooper came down and rescued us. Tom wasn't bothered, just bewildered, and when we sat at the table the lunch party was in full swing. Anecdotes, yarns, lies were being bandied across the table – everybody was in good spirits, laughing and looking at Tom, waiting hopefully for him to contribute with a funny episode.

Tom, however, was enjoying the food and when the crowd had given up on his contribution, he put down his knife and fork and rose from his chair and lay flat on the floor for a couple of minutes, then he got up, sat down and continued his lunch. All the other diners looked at each other in amazement. When they drifted back into their own conversations I asked Tom quietly, 'What was all that about?'

He swallowed his mouthful and said, 'I just thought I'd do something visual.'

By this time Tom was bowing to the inevitable, the audiences had decided long ago, unanimously, that comedy was his forté.

When Tom first had ambitions for a stage career, comedy wasn't even on his agenda. His sights were set on being the best magician, conjurer, illusionist in the world and to this end he practised religiously throughout his life. It is easy to overlook the fact that he was not only a member of the Magic Circle, he was a member of the Inner Circle, and you have to be something special to be elected to this extremely exclusive sect.

Privately, his tricks round a table, closely watched by friends, were incredible. So brilliantly executed it was indeed magical. The number of times I've sat next to him, I never once saw him do the same trick twice and even had he presented any one of his illusions twenty times, I would not have the faintest idea how it was done – and I watched him as closely as a hovering kestrel with a mouse on the menu.

It is incredible to think of Tommy Cooper paralysing his audiences every night with his simple magical disasters then returning home, practising half the night on another mind-blowing piece of magic that even old Merlin wouldn't be able to fathom.

And lastly, back to his comedy. On stage it was hilarious and never in all his career did he mouth a swear word, a sexist or racist joke, or a double entendre or a lavatorial sequence. In my opinion, there is yet to emerge a comedian better. Perhaps there is a lesson here.

Dear Tom, I will always remember your lovely lost expression. That typified his awkwardness, coupled with a fez that on Tom's head looked more like a red thimble with a tassel. Incidentally, Tom's son gave me the fez after Tom died.

'My father would have liked you to have this,' he said. It is on my mantelpiece reminding me always of my favourite Comedy Hero.

LES DAWSON

Novelist, poet and philosopher of fun

PROFILE

Born: 2 February 1931

Place of birth: Collyhurst, Manchester

A former jazz pianist with the Cotton City Slickers, Les made ends meet, while playing the Northern club circuit as a comic, by selling everything from vacuum cleaners to toilet brushes. Despairing of ever making the big time, he appeared on *Opportunity Knocks* in 1967 and became an instant hit.

Selected TV: *Sez Les* (1969-76), *Dawson's Weekly* (1975), *The Loner* (1975), *The Les Dawson Show* (1978-89), *The Dawson Watch* (1978-80), *Blankety Blank* (1984-90), *Opportunity Knocks* (host, 1990)

Died: 10 June 1993

If ever there were such a thing as a 'born comedian' it would have to be Les Dawson. Most children at birth have old, wizened faces, but in a short time they tend to grow out of this awkward start in life. However, Les Dawson must have by-passed this natural transformation; he didn't grow out of it. On the contrary, it is my belief he grew into it. I came to this assumption on our first meeting when I looked into his face.

Les was as Lancashire as 'hotpot' and some of his patter was earthy, as familiar as a stick of Blackpool Rock and saucy postcards, but he introduced what had hitherto been a parochial sense of humour to the whole country via television. There must have been Southerners who would laugh, not quite knowing why but they couldn't wait for another helping on his next television show.

His description of his mother-in-law approaching him on Blackpool sands: 'I knew it was her. Only she could plod like that with a donkey under each arm.'

This, however, was only one facet of his wit – he would sometimes sprinkle in his 'bread-pudding' humour with lyrical lines of melancholy. In one of his soliloquies he spoke of going down the yard to the outdoor privy and, as he sat there, he happened to gaze up at a hole in the roof and here he described the night, the blackness, millions of stars, the galaxy, the great universal unknown. (This I must add was a poetic description much better than I can put down on paper.) Les delivered all this in a soft, wondering, rasping tone bringing us down to earth with, 'And I thought to myself – I must get that hole mended.' Yes, there was a poet in Les Dawson, not only struggling to get out but succeeding, much to our delight.

He was old when I first gazed into his multi-lined face, but I doubt if he was yet forty – just about the time when a normal person studies closely in the mirror his first wrinkle. Here was dear old Les with a face full of 500 years of suffering, but make no mistake, behind that facade of misery his brain sparkled like the 'Kohinoor' diamond.

I don't think Les ever considered being a comedian when he finished his National Service. I have the feeling he didn't quite know which direction to take or where his future lay – certainly not in a shop, or an office or, God forbid, a cotton mill! So he chose another path. He wrote a novel, which must have been good – it was published. With the first step in his career imprinted in the sand, assured of his place in the literary world, he made his way to Paris; the Left Bank, no less, home of all creation – Jean-Paul Sartre, Hemingway and now Dawson.

However, one novel doesn't make a writer and the muse was on holiday. Sadly, croissants, red wine and an attic don't grow on trees. So, in order to afford the bare essentials, he took a job as a pianist in a club, tinkling melodies while customers staggered up to him placing a bottle of lager on top of the piano in appreciation and Did he know 'I'll Walk Alone'? There Les went one better than Jean- Paul and Hemingway. As far as I know, neither of them played the piano. However, poor Les was under a misapprehension; he thought he was in a club, it turned out to be a brothel. But, quite honestly, if you're going to play the piano in a brothel what better place than Paris and what better grounding for a budding comedian?

Years later, when I first met him, he was well established in the comedy hierarchy with one Royal Variety Performance under his belt. He played himself in one of my television shows with Hattie. Later, we shared a caravan together, which was our dressing room, when we appeared in a Royal Charity event in Windsor Great Park. The Queen and Prince Philip were highly amused and even great-great-grandmother, Victoria, would have been amused by Les's antics. To cap it all, Les and I appeared together in a play in a summer season at Blackpool and, as that is where he lived, I enjoyed many a breakfast at his home, followed by a hilarious game of golf.

All our meetings, either socially or professionally, were like a holiday for me. Two hours in his company did me more good than two months on a health farm – incidentally I've never been to a health farm, why should I when Les was around?

So, as you will understand, I spent quite a bit of time with him. However, in spite of our many get-togethers, I never really got to know him. I believe few people did. But all who knew him shared a common bond – we thoroughly enjoyed his company.

Theatricals are like ships that pass in the night. There is a metaphorical likeness here. There are the sleek, ocean-going liners – the maritime Terry Thomas. On the other hand, the doughty, little steamers taking passengers to and from New Brighton to the Isle of Man in all weathers, buffeting sturdily through choppy waters, this would define Les Dawson.

I base this analogy on one of my fond memories of Les in flat cap, strutting down the fairway following his stomach, whilst pulling his golf trolley loaded with a set of unmatched golf clubs he must have bought as a job lot.

As one philosopher put it, 'The eyes are the windows to the soul.' In which case, to look into Les Dawson's tired old eyes one can only assume he had a tired old soul which could at one time have belonged to Plato or Wordsworth.

He did everything with a weary air of triumph, even getting out of a chair was an effort but to all who were close to him we could only applaud the fact that he'd made the effort in order to entertain us.

KEN DODD

Night worker in a jam butty factory

PROFILE

Born: 8 November 1927

Place of birth: Knotty Ash, Liverpool

Ken started out as a ventriloquist before deciding that his distinctive buck teeth (the result of a childhood cycling accident) were better suited to crazy comedy. After amateur appearances as Professor Yaffle Chuckabutty – Operatic Tenor and Sausage Knotter, he turned professional in 1954.

Selected radio: *The Ken Dodd Show* (1963-79), *Doddy's Daft Half Hour* (1972), *Doddy's Comic Cuts* (1973), *Doddy's World of Whimsy* (1975)

Selected TV: *The Ken Dodd Show* (1960-69), *Doddy's Music Box* (1967-68), *Ken Dodd and the Diddymen* (1969-72), *Funny You Should Say That* (1972), *Ken Dodd's World of Laughter* (1975-76), *Ken Dodd's Showbiz* (1982), *An Audience with Ken Dodd* (1994)

I never understood how anyone could listen to Ken Dodd's show on the wireless and not be uplifted by Ken's exuberant zest for life in which a shining sun is a permanent feature.

To me his half-hour was a tonic or, to put it another way, it saved me a fortune in doctor's bills. For example, who else could declaim, 'What a lovely day for running through Sainsbury's shouting "Waitrose!"' It's not much in written form, but delivered by the irrepressible Ken Dodd it takes on a glorious insight into a child's interpretation of anarchy.

Once, when I was appearing in Blackpool with my old friend Jimmy Edwards, I was delighted to hear that Ken Dodd was starring in another theatre just up the road. As we hadn't yet opened, I knew where my treat for that night was coming from. Jim might come as well, although I wasn't too hopeful. He would never go to a theatre unless he happened to be working there, but when I told him it was Ken Dodd he broke the rule of a lifetime and together we entered the front of the theatre, which was a novelty for Jim. The show had already started and the first thing I noticed in the box office was that all the windows were closed which was hardly surprising as there wasn't an empty seat in the house.

Jim suggested that, as Ken wouldn't be on till the second half, we could nip across the road to the pub then come back in about an hour. I wasn't overjoyed. If Jim got settled with a large whisky we might well miss the show altogether. In fact, we might well miss the next three performances. So I compromised.

'Let's nip upstairs to the theatre bar,' I said. 'We can slip in after the interval.' Jim agreed, rubbing his hands together in anticipation, but at that moment the theatre manager appeared and, on recognising us, apologised

that there wasn't a seat and if only we'd let him know
. . . he looked so miserable I said, 'Cheer up, at least
you've got a full house.'

He looked at me in surprise and said, 'I'm not worried
about the audience, what bothers me is how long is Ken
going to do. He was on for three hours last night!'

Then I understood his predicament. Ken's propensity
to go on long after his allotted time was legendary in the
profession. When I asked Ken later about this he said, 'As
long as they're enjoying it, so am I,' a philosophy I find
that reveals the character of the man. All I have is yours
. . . no wonder he is a legend.

After a few noggins and an interval, Jim and I stood
at the back to watch the second half. Ken did exceed
his scheduled time but no one in the audience was
complaining and after two hours people were leaving to
catch their last buses home, eyes streaming, still laughing
as they backed up the aisle reluctant to leave the 'King'.
What a presence, what timing and what laughs. Half an
hour later he said to the audience, 'Do you give in?' They
roared with laughter, hardly a line to merit a reaction
but delivered with complete guilelessness and he did
another twenty minutes.

Today he would be put in the category of 'stand-up
comic', what a puerile description, 'stand-up comic', as
if there were 'lying-down comics', or even 'sitting-down'
comics.

Ken's creation of 'The Diddymen' was a masterstroke,
bouncing little tots dancing with joyful energy, evoking
the envy of many a child in the audience . . . not forget-
ting grown-ups who remember their own childhood with
fond nostalgia.

Jim and I were captivated and I suggested we go round
the back to let Ken know what a fantastic evening it had

been. Then I wondered if Jim would be too tired, after all, like me, he had stood throughout the performance. Until I remembered he was an expert at standing for hours, as many a landlord will tell you. We went backstage and found we couldn't get near Ken's dressing room – the passage was jammed full of wheelchairs. It was like Lourdes on an Easter bank holiday. It was fully twenty minutes before we went in and there was the maestro, sweat dripping from him onto a towel round his neck. It was very humbling to think that Ken had not only done over three hours on a hot stage, he'd spent another hour in his dressing room entertaining his disabled admirers. It's a side of him the public rarely sees.

We meet every time I go to Liverpool and I've done many plays in the city. I have to go to Liverpool because he rarely comes to London and when he does it's never more than a day. Like most Northerners, he's wary of the South. I can understand his unease. He is, without doubt, the finest comedian in this country today, but he still lives in Knotty Ash – not for him the lure of the tinsel facade of Los Angeles or Las Vegas, Lake Tahore and other night spots. His feet are firmly planted in Knotty Ash, same house, same Liverpool skyline and as long as I've known him, same suit – and that's Ken, a man I look up to and revere. If I find a restaurant which serves jam butties I'll invite him to tea. After all, wasn't the jam butty factory one of his creations?

I don't think Ken realises the enormous following he has or how great his popularity. If he does, he accepts it with humility and a little surprise. For instance, this year, when I was at the Playhouse Theatre in Chekhov's *The Three Sisters*, I had a surprise visitor after the show. It was Ken and his wife Ann. They apologised for their lateness. I don't know why they had to be apologetic; they were late because at the stage door Ken had been besieged by fans outside waiting for our autographs. When the rushers-off of our cast reached the stage door, they saw the mob and in the middle, signing furiously, was Ken Dodd. Delighted, they returned and stood outside their dressing rooms and when Ken eventually came down he was besieged again by our company. By the time the cast left Ken and Ann with me and made their way out of the stage door there was not a soul to be seen. All the autograph hunters had gone home, hugging their books and even programmes of our show but most importantly bearing the signature of Ken Dodd.

I had quite a few famous friends visiting me at the theatre but none, so far as I know, with the exception of John Williams, received the admiration and attention paid to Ken Dodd.

Finally, to all young and old aspiring comedians, you would be well advised to study, watch and learn from Ken Dodd, the Master Craftsman. Well advised.

CHARLIE DRAKE

A big man in a little body

PROFILE

Born: (Charles Springall) 19 June 1925

Place of Birth: South London

The son of a newspaper seller, Charlie went into show business as a singer before turning to comedy. His big break was appearing with Bob Monkhouse and Dennis Goodwin in *Fast and Loose*, during which Monkhouse accidentally blew off Charlie's left ear with a blank bullet.

Selected films: *Sands of the Desert* (1960), *Petticoat Pirates* (1961), *The Cracksman* (1963), *Mister Ten Percent* (1966)

Selected TV: *Mick and Montmorency* (1956-58), *Drake's Progress* (1957-58), *The Charlie Drake Show* (1960-1), *The Worker* (1965-70), *Who is Sylvia?* (1967), *Slapstick and Old Lace* (1971), *The Plank* (1979)

Charlie Drake, chubby, small, curly blond hair set back on his cherubic fizzog, every grandmother's dream of a grandson . . . first choice in a film about the choirboys of St Paul's . . . this guileless innocence attracted millions of viewers every week to his TV show, *The Worker*, aided or more likely hampered, by my old friend Henry McGee as a harassed official in the Labour Exchange.

Just to watch happy little Charlie entering his office only to meet the long, doleful, 'why does it always happen to me?' face of Henry McGee knowing full well his peaceful day was about to be blown out of the water was worth the price of the licence fee; just for this moment.

From the start of the series I knew with no doubt at all that Charlie was a major player in the comedy industry. His 'Hello my darlings' became the catch phrase of the nation and, although catch phrases have never been my favourite means of getting a laugh, I make an exception with 'Hello my darlings' coming from Charlie. It wasn't a bad introduction and from then on the creation of his character was well on the way. Everything about him seems to fit his voice, his figure and most of all that disarming air of trust emanating from him. At every opportunity I cast Charlie in my silent films, he was the answer to any director's dream, it was his timing, the quickness of his mind in grasping an intricate move. A perfect one-take man, the second take for the crew's amusement.

I met Charlie mainly on the golf courses and he was pretty useful too, straight down the middle of the fairway, thank God he wasn't often in the rough, never mind his ball, we might never have found him.

In all the years I played golf with him he always kept his cool, should he miss the ball altogether he would calmly assert it was a practice swing. On the rare occasions when he did hit his ball into the trees he would march in after it, and in a moment or two the ball would fly back to the middle of the fairway. Once when he marched into the trees he forgot to take a club with him, but the ball still sailed out onto the fairway, he simply smiled serenely, and one didn't have the heart to ask awkward questions. However, make no mistake, underneath that air of butter being OK in his mouth, he was as tough as a billiard table leg and not much taller, as Stanley Baker found to his cost.

Stanley, one of our great film actors, a real hard case, was usually cast as the villain. He was a good mate; later he received a well-deserved Knighthood. However, in those days, when we were all commoners, there was a group of us keen avid golfers: Sean Connery, Stanley Baker, Ronnie Carroll, Charlie and myself and one or two others. In between filming, televising, staging, there were enough of us on the golf course to win or lose a few quid because Stanley Baker was a betting man and his roll of white fivers made my five bob look ridiculous. On this particular day we had four matches and the leading one was Stanley against Charlie . . . naturally, they'd both backed themselves to win, no half-crown bets for them, or even five pounds. I never found out what the bet was but I'm sure it would have purchased a small bijou residence.

They strode over to the first tee and the game commenced. Charlie with his innocent smile and Stanley, nostrils white, clutching his driver like a murder weapon. When he addressed the ball he glared at it as if it had sinned against him; he didn't just strike the ball he punished it. No wonder several of his drives ended up in the deep woods but to my knowledge he never seemed to lose one, neither did Charlie. Anyway, as this is not a book about golf, suffice to say Charlie won the match on the sixteenth hole, three up and only two to play. Stanley was furious, he couldn't believe he'd lost and to Charlie, who didn't even come up to his belt buckle. However, Stanley hadn't finished. For those of you unfamiliar with the foibles of golf, it is sometimes customary for the loser to suggest a 'bye'. In this case Stanley, having lost the match on the sixteenth hole, was asking Charlie if he would continue to play the last two holes. If Stanley lost again he would not only lose his initial stake but would have to pay Charlie half as much again. On the other hand, if Charlie won Stanley would be liable to his original stake and half that on top. If I have not made this quite clear, any respectable golf club will explain but please, I beg of you, don't mention my name.

To get back to the anecdote, Stanley, the inveterate gambler, was sure that he could save half of his original stake. After all, the seventeenth was a par five and it would probably take Charlie six shots even to reach the green whereas Stanley, being nearly three foot taller, should be able to make it in three. It was going to be a walkover. Alas, there was a fly in the Germoline. Charlie flatly refused Stanley his 'bye', explaining that he'd flogged himself to death in order to win and he was not prepared to risk half the bet on the last two holes. Stanley, staring down into the calm, unruffled, stubborn gaze was infuriated. Charlie, unmoved, stared innocently up into the steaming nostrils above him and shook his head. All through this altercation I was waiting to play my second shot into the green but Stanley and Charlie were obviously locked into some kind of drama. They were impervious to my shouts of 'Fore'. From a distance it looked as if Stanley was talking to a sunflower, then he snatched up his bag and strode furiously back to the clubhouse.

Whatever the trouble was, Charlie was the winner but the drama was far from over. Stanley, bless him, never lost a bet if he could help it. Like a dog with a bone he worried it until he'd extracted all the meat. So, sidling up to Charlie at the bar with the smile of a crocodile about to snap off your leg, he asked Charlie if he'd like a return match on the following day. Charlie agreed and together they had a drink. Charlie wasn't bothered. He would be playing with Stanley's money anyway.

On the morrow, when they'd finished their return match, I happened to walk into the locker room, empty except for Charlie sitting in his underpants and singlet gazing at nothing in particular.

'Hello, Charlie,' I said. 'How did you get on?'

'You'll never guess,' he replied, smiling. 'We got to the sixteenth hole which I won, and the match.'

'Did you have a "bye"?' I asked.

He shook his head. 'Stanley was just about to bring it up when I stopped him.' He shook his head again and in his high singsong voice he said, 'We're not having a "bye" Stanley and I thought I made that clear yesterday and just one other thing,' he said chuckling 'don't snatch up your bag and walk back again you look such a prat.'

Stanley was a big man and knew when he was beaten. He shook hands with Charlie and played the last holes in. It was only later we found out that Stanley had won a big bet he'd placed backing Charlie to win. It's a funny old world but, needless to say, Stanley never played Charlie again, being content to take his money off me.

Charlie's career was blossoming; he was making films, recording songs and appearing at the Palladium, the Mecca of all comedians, but unfortunately it is always the one day you don't take out your umbrella when you're hit by a cloudburst. Charlie was about to star in a

pantomime and gave one of the principal parts to a girl
he knew. She had talent, she had looks, in fact she had
everything except an Equity Card. In those days it was a
catch 22 situation; if you hadn't got an Equity Card you
couldn't work but you had to work in order to apply for
an Equity Card.

Charlie, stubborn as a brick wall, flatly refused
to replace the girl and by doing what I consider the
honourable thing, virtually put the brakes on his
own career. Equity applied the muscle and Charlie
suddenly found work offers drying up. He never once
complained nor bemoaned the change in his fortunes
but I am certain that we lost a genuine creative
comedian.

Every time we meet he always wears a smile. He is
older now, but in fact he looks as he was forty years ago.
I applaud his courage and determination – there aren't
many people who will put their career on the line for a
principle. It may appear to some foolhardy but for myself
he has all my admiration and I am grateful to call him a
friend.

JIMMY EDWARDS

High-flyer with laughter in his heart

PROFILE

Born: 23 March 1920

Place of Birth: Barnes, London

Jimmy studied at Cambridge having gone there on a choral scholarship before being called up into the RAF during WWII and serving as a pilot. He was awarded the DFC for his bravery over Arnhem and had to have plastic surgery which he disguised with his trademark handlebar moustache.

Selected radio: *Take It From Here, Hancock's Half Hour*

Selected films: *Trouble in the Air* (1948), *Helter Skelter* (1949), *Mystery at the Burlesque* (1950), *Treasure Hunt* (1952), *An Alligator Named Daisy* (1955), *Three Men in a Boat* (1956), *Bottoms Up* (1960), *The Plank* (1967), *Lionheart* (1968), *The Bed Sitting Room* (1969)

Selected TV: *Whacko!* (1956-60, 1971), *Does the Team Think?* (1958), *John Jorrocks Esq.* (1959), *Seven Faces of Jim* (1961), *Bold as Brass* (1964), *Blandings Castle* (1967), *The Fossett Saga* (1969), *Take It From Here* (1978)

Died: 7 July 1988

James Keith O'Neil Edwards would often introduce himself as Professor Jimmy Edwards, MA, CANTAB, Failed MP, but I will always remember him simply as 'dear old Jim'.

Born in Barnes at the end of World War I, he was determined to get into the next one. In all the years we toured together in *Big Bad Mouse* I never once heard him sing or hum a note, which is surprising as he spent his early formative years as a choir boy – in St Paul's, no less! Educated at Cambridge, he graduated with a Master of Arts degree and he was all set for the big time. He tossed a coin; Prime Minister or the Archbishop of Canterbury? But, like many of my Comedy Heroes, World War II intervened and his career move for the next six years was already decided.

For the most part, he once told me, his war was a doddle. I was sceptical because Jim was an RAF pilot, even getting some of those old planes in the air would scarcely be described as a doddle. However, the way Jim told it he seemed to have found a cushy billet. He spent most of his war in Toronto, Canada, flying trainee navigators who worked at their charts, giving Jim the correct course to bring them back to the airfield. He told me of one occasion when the young would-be navigator panicked and completely muffed his plotting. This was serious, if he lost his head over a training flight what might he do in a future bombing raid over Berlin? OK to follow my leader on the way in, but on the return trip to find the sky empty of other 'friendlies', a panic with his figures, eventually bringing them to a landing strip in Essen instead of Essex . . . it was only a hypothesis, but I saw Jim's point. He went on, the trainee was a gibbering wreck when Jim pretended to panic as well, moaning that they were running out of fuel flying willy-nilly through a coal black sky.

Although they were still some distance away from the airfield, Jim, underneath his mad panic routine, was completely unruffled. It wasn't too surprising because Canada was not a blacked out land like most of Europe. Toronto was lit up and especially Yonge Street. This was a boon to Jim as Yonge Street is about a thousand miles long, straight as an arrow and, would you believe, the end of this direct route ended at Jim's airfield! One can imagine his false relief as he pointed down to the landing strip. I've no doubt Jim would probably have said something like, 'Well, we were lucky this time,' before helping the distressed navigator to his hut in case he couldn't find it. Incidentally, Jim added, two weeks later the would-be navigator was on his way back to England.

For most people who enjoy flying, and especially pilots, it is not just an occupation, it is an addiction and to Jim his two great passions were horse riding and easing back the stick to coax his beloved Dakotas into whatever was up there. Luckily, the skies over Toronto were not hostile, apart from the weather, and if that was dicey the flyers had a day off. Another drop of unbelievably good fortune for Jim was that Alan Edwards, Jim's elder brother, who was also in the RAF, was stationed on the same airfield. I met Alan several years later, after the war, when Jim and I were touring together and it always seemed to me that Alan was still looking after Jim, worrying when Jim was down, happy when he smiled, running their farm, looking forward to Jim's infrequent visits, marvelling at his younger brother's vitality and exuberance.

Jim had a colossal appetite for life and while he was stuffing himself, Alan would be content with a mouthful of bread and cheese in the background. In those halcyon wartime days in Toronto, it was Alan who procured a horse so that Jim could indulge his hobby when not on duty, galloping off into the wild blue yonder and, believe me, there is an awful lot of wild blue yonder in Canada. Which reminds me, Jim passed a billboard in Toronto – 'Drink Canada Dry' and Jim, who loved his tipple, turned to Alan and wryly observed, 'I'm doing my best.'

It all reads like an idyllic life for Jim and he admits it was. After all, he was a first-class RAF pilot and he'd never fired a gun or dropped a bomb. I think his worst accident occurred when he fell off his horse! One must understand, however, that Jim didn't engineer this cushy billet. There was no string pulling to have Alan posted with him. Had he been assigned to Whitleys or Blenheims or any other early widow makers, he wouldn't have argued, he wouldn't be too exhilarated either, but you went where you were posted and Jim drew the lucky straw.

But, like all good things, it came to an end. In Jim's case it didn't just end, it ran slap bang into the buffers. His rude awakening came on receiving a summons to report to the C.O. I will attempt to recreate the interview as faithfully as Jim recounted it.

'Ah, good morning, Edwards.'

'Good morning, Sir.'

'You've done sterling work on the station and we have all enjoyed your company.'

Pause whilst the C.O. filled his pipe and Jim desperately tried to put a brake on his sinking stomach.

The C.O. went on: 'We'll miss you, of course.'

Jim's brakes almost failed him.

'However, no doubt you're champing on the bit to get back to the real war?'

'Oh, yes, Sir,' Jim enthusiastically lied.

'Good man,' said the C.O. 'I wish I was going with you.'

Jim thought, 'I wished he was going instead of me.'

A few weeks later, back in England, a blacked-out war zone with no lit up Yonge Street to guide him home, he was glad of a refresher course in his beloved Dakotas.

The Dakota was a friendly aircraft – reliable, trustworthy, no unexpected tricks up its honest fuselage, a grand old workhorse but hardly an offensive weapon. It did not carry bombs, had no guns (unless you count the one that greased the axles), it simply carried supplies or VIPs from here to there. This did not exempt it, however, from becoming a target for anti-aircraft batteries, enemy fighter planes, or any other hazards of aerial warfare. The Dakota was an old lady plodding steadfastly through a minefield with fingers crossed, but Jim enjoyed every take-off and landing and any nearby pub.

The good times Jim had enjoyed in Canada didn't come free, though. There was a price to be paid and Jim received the bill as he flew over the coast of England to the real War – his destination was Arnhem. He glanced around him at other Dakotas towing gliders to the killing ground of the little Dutch town; as they approached the target it is not difficult to imagine Jim's dry mouth in his baptism of fire. Dirty black blobs of anti-aircraft batteries, slow moving tracers, explosions rocking the aircraft, it was a death trap ringed by heavy German reinforcements. Due to leaked intelligence, the whole of the airborne assault force dropping slowly to earth were sitting ducks for the German gunners. It was one of the disasters of the war.

The Dakotas flew into that awesome ring of fire, released their gliders and the lucky ones turned back for Blighty to be hitched onto another glider to make the return trip into the inferno. Jim didn't mention any of this, they are entirely from my own imagination. All he said was, 'We were towing gliders full of airborne troops to Arnhem and when I released my glider I banked on a course that would take me back to England and put the plane onto automatic pilot then I took up my thermos of coffee . . .'

Incidentally, Jim was telling me this as if he were describing a picnic at Henley but I urged him to go on. Over to Jim: 'I was just about to unscrew the cup from my Thermos when I spotted a dot ahead growing larger every second, an aircraft, and suddenly there was a twinkling of lights along the leading edge of the wing. Then it zoomed over the Dakota, which was now on fire having taken several hits.'

Jim flicked off 'George', the automatic pilot, but the Dakota was mortally wounded. He ordered his crew to bail out. Jim chuckled ruefully when he told me this. Apparently, after despatching his crew, he realised he had left it too late to bail out himself so he was left with no alternative than to try and land what was left of his darling Dakota. Thank God Jim was a very experienced pilot.

I may have misheard him but, with flames all round, when he landed what was left of the old Dakota he was still desperately endeavouring to fly it while standing on the burning seat. Jim, with his flying suit scorched and half his ear burnt away, staggered into a ditch expecting the arrival of German soldiers attracted by the pall of black smoke from the dying Dakota. But the Dutch Resistance got there before them and when Jim recovered consciousness, he was lying bandaged in a Dutch hospital. There was obviously a lot he didn't tell me but it must have been quite a heroic turn of events because he was awarded the Distinguished Flying Cross. Jim was evacuated to hospital in Blighty and by the time he was passed fit for duty the war was over and he was a civilian once more.

Fortunately, during Jim's time in Canada, where he organised and appeared in many a show for the airfield personnel, he made the joyful discovery he had a talent for making audiences laugh. He knew now in which direction his career would be heading.

His first appearance was at the Windmill Theatre, a Mecca for all the newly demobbed servicemen putting forward a tentative step into comedy. The Windmill was notorious for its nudes, comely young ladies posing in the buff, not allowed to move by law. It was a difficult job where even a sneeze could close the theatre. There were six performances a day and sadly the audience was usually of the grubby mac brigade, gaping and slobbering at the naked girls in frozen tableau. They could have seen the same thing in any art gallery, and for free. When the curtain dropped and a new comic entered, newspapers in the audience were raised as the heavy breathers made their racing selections, presenting four minutes of silence to a depressed young hopeful.

Jim suffered all these indignities with his hilarious musical act but he was determined . . . he hadn't won his DFC for nothing. Performance after performance he suffered the indifference but he had not gone unnoticed and his big break came in 1948 in *Take it From Here* with Joy Nicholls and Dick Bentley, written by Frank Muir and Denis Norden. Almost from its inception *T.I.F.H.* was a success. The show featured a family sit-com, The Glums, with Jimmy as the loud Father Glum, Dick Bentley as his thick-as-a-club-sandwich son Ron, and June Whitfield as Ron's whining girlfriend Eth. I still remember some of the brilliant lines. In one scene Jim wants to keep his son Ron indoors and Ron is desperate to think of an excuse to go out for a tryst with Eth. An idea occurs to Ron, 'Dad,' he whines, 'I think I'll walk down to the Post Office. I feel like a tuppeny-ha'penny stamp.'

I can still enjoy listening in my mind to this day. It was *Take It From Here* that put Jim firmly on the Yellow Brick Road to stardom and booted him into the upper echelons of comedy.

Following his early radio success, Jimmy starred in the Adelphi Theatre with Tony Hancock, Dick Bentley and Joy Nicholls. Now not only was his foot on the ladder he was climbing in through the top window.

My father came down from Oldham to pay me a visit and I took him to the Adelphi to see the show. To say that my father enjoyed watching Jim was a gross understatement; he was mesmerised like a child on his first visit to the fairy grotto, and when I took him round the back to introduce him to Jim, his cup was overflowing. The three of us sat down to late night dinner; it was hilarious. Jim was on form and the food was good although my father didn't eat a lot – he was laughing too much and afraid his teeth might fall out.

On the morrow when I saw him on to the train at Euston he said, 'I came down to see the sights of London.'

I said, 'I'm sorry, Dad, you've only seen Jim.' He was amazed.

'Don't be sorry, lad,' he said. 'One hour with Jim is worth a guided tour round Buckingham Palace and tea with the Queen thrown in.' Then the train began to move.

Years later, my telephone rang. It was Jim and without any preamble he said, 'Michael Codron is putting on a comedy play. Six weeks touring the provinces then we go into the West End. I've agreed to do it if you will.'

I didn't hesitate. 'OK,' I said. 'If you've already agreed to do it, I'll be delighted to join you,'

'Good,' he said. 'I'll tell Michael.'

He was about to hang up when I said, 'By the way, Jim, what's the play about?'

'No idea,' he said. 'I haven't read it yet.'

Perhaps we should have, but we had great faith in Michael Codron, a highly respected impresario to this day. He must have read the play, entitled *Big Bad Mouse*, and decided the partnership of Jim and I would be worth the risk. I've no idea where we played our first date. The mind is a wonderful creation, it forgets things that are horrendous. Week two was no better – I think the usherettes outnumbered the audience.

After the fifth week Jim and I agreed the mistake we were making was obvious . . . we were doing the play. The sixth and final week was at the Palace Theatre, Manchester. Monday night same disaster, where the cast outnumbered the audience even though it was pouring with rain outside. It was then that Jim and I decided that the play should have been given the last rites before it reached the publishers and we had edged it further into the realms of banality by attempting to act it, especially as neither of us had had the benefit of RADA.

Jim came into my dressing room, a large whisky in his hand, 'Well, Eric,' he said, 'it's obvious we'll not be going into the West End so I'm going to have a bit of fun.'

Together we clinked glasses and I said, 'Well, Jim, if you're going to have fun, so am I,' and to a very small collection of theatre buffs Jim kicked the ball into play and the game was afoot. In the scene Jim was drinking a hefty glass of cold tea whilst smoking a cheroot. This was where the play ended and the fun began. Jim left his desk and came forward to lean on the proscenium arch and addressed the audience directly.

He said, 'You'd think on our last week they'd give me real whisky,' then he looked at his cheroot with some disdain, 'and a real cigar.' And then it was my turn: 'I wish they'd give me a real actor.' And the people laughed and applauded – that was all the encouragement we needed. From then on we were hell bent on anarchy.

Unbeknown to us, Frankie Howerd had been in the audience and when he came round the back to see us, he said it was the funniest show he'd ever seen and with a shrug of resignation he said, 'But I would have liked to have seen the play.'

However, much to our delight, the audiences at the Palace Theatre increased enormously, phones ringing persistently in the Box Office, even the manager came to the dressing room to ask how we were.

On the last night, Michael Codron came up to Manchester to have a commiserating drink with us, a magnanimous gesture as he obviously lost money on the tour. He was in for a shock – a pleasant one – and an evening no one could have foreseen. To begin with, when he arrived at the Theatre it was pandemonium. Mounted police tried to control the crowds outside the theatre because, according to the Box Office, they had had to turn more than a thousand people away and, unfortunately, such was the chaos that poor old Michael couldn't get in to see the show.

Having a farewell drink with him afterwards, it was a happy drink when Michael had prepared for a wake. Again Jim, ever the prophet and with a university education behind him, said, 'Well, Mike, old cock, if you take us off now you want your head testing.' Michael didn't even visit the doctor for a second opinion, in two weeks' time we opened in the West End at the Shaftesbury Theatre where the play ran successfully for eighteen months. From the Shaftesbury Theatre we simply used the play as a vehicle for our double act.

Paul Elliott, another of our favourite impresarios, took over the show which, in the next twenty odd years, toured the world. When either Jim or I were at a loose end all we had to do was ring Paul Elliott and in a few days we'd be off to Australia, Hong Kong, America, in fact we enjoyed a very hilarious mystery tour whenever we both happened to be free. The play gained the sobriquet 'the most successful flop in theatre history' and when we finally put it to bed we were on our seventeenth farewell tour.

Denis Norden and I frequently discuss you, Jim, with a happy nostalgia that keeps you always in our memories.

BILL FRASER

Bags of talent, sacks of stamina, but all out of luck

PROFILE

Born: 5 June 1908

Place of birth: Perth, Scotland

Originally a bank clerk by profession, Bill persuaded his parents to let him to go to London and become an actor at the age of 24. Before his stage career took off, he was so poor that by night he was reduced to sleeping on the Embankment.

Selected theatre: *The Farmer's Wife* (1967), *Twelfth Night* (1969), *Mrs Warren's Profession* (1970), *Uncle Vanya* (1982)

Selected films: *Orders Are Orders* (1954), *Masquerade* (1965), *A Home of Your Own* (1965), *Up the Chastity Belt* (1971)

Selected TV: *And So to Bentley* (1954), *The Army Game* (1957-61), *Bootsie and Snudge* (1960-63, 1974), *Foreign Affairs* (1964), *That's Your Funeral* (1971), *The Train Now Standing* (1972-73), *Rhubarb Rhubarb!* (1980), *Doctor's Daughters* (1981), *The Secret Diary of Adrian Mole, Aged 13¾* (1985-87)

Died: 5 September 1987

It has been said that, in order to succeed as an actor, the most important assets are stamina, talent and luck. Bill Fraser undoubtedly had stamina, he was blessed with enormous talent, but unfortunately where Bill was concerned luck seemed to glance the other way.

In 1939, a show opened in the West End of London entitled *New Faces*. It wasn't the usual revue type: dancing, singing and satire dominating the lighter side of theatre. *New Faces* was an apt title because, when boiled down, it was an upmarket talent show. New young comedians given the chance to display their comedic talents to a critical jury, the audience. Bill Fraser was one of the hopefuls and, as if to contradict my earlier assumption that luck ignored Bill, he won the contest hands down.

For Bill it was 'Open Sesame' to the big time, he was not only on the first rung to stardom, he was halfway up the ladder, his future assured . . . but was it? We're all aware of the pitfalls of counting one's chickens, and luck at its most capricious, pulled the ladder from under Bill. It was September the third, the day war was declared, and Bill, being the right age at the wrong time, was called up.

What cruel irony. Instead of his name in lights he found himself in the Royal Air Force in a blackout. However, there was still hope. Optimistically, it would all be over by Christmas. Sadly, it wasn't. The war went on for another six years. After the cessation of hostilities in 1945, Bill, like everyone else in uniform, was hanging around waiting for demob. He was under no illusion . . . he would not be able to pick up where he left off in 1939. He would not be remembered, but Bill had not forgotten how to entertain and he proved it. He produced and starred in three revues written by Ron Rich and our own Denis Norden: *Bags of Panic, It's in the Bag* and lastly, *Three Bags Full*, after which Bill and Denis were demobbed. I was in those shows and even then Bill was the 'governor'. To see him on stage was a salutary reminder of the gulf between amateur and professional; he was a great teacher by example.

Some time later I was a civilian myself, but with a difference. I'd been bitten by the theatre bug. Unfortunately, it didn't show from the front, so I didn't get much work round and about Oldham. There was only one thing for it – I arrived in London and, not unnaturally, nothing had changed except that London is bigger than Oldham. After a week, hungry, no money, no hope, I was walking disconsolately along the Embankment. It was a silent, bitterly cold night. London was shrouded in an impenetrable pea-soup fog, no traffic, no people. I was in a miserable world of my own but it was while in these depths of despair that a shadow passed by and then I heard a voice: 'Eric,' it said. I was so down that for a moment I thought it was the 'Grim Reaper'. What happened next is incredible but absolutely true. Out of nine million strangers in London it turned out to be Bill Fraser.

He was starring at The Playhouse Theatre in a revue called *Between Ourselves*. Starring no less! And as I sat in a comfy chair in his dressing room, I must have looked to Bill as if I had one foot in the knacker's yard, and he wouldn't have been too far off the mark. So, coming to a decision, he asked me would I like to write for him?

Naturally, with only one penny in my pocket, I said 'Yes.' I would have said yes to anything, even if he'd asked me to give him a piggy back up the Strand. In fact, he employed me for three weeks in which time he never asked me to write anything, which was just as well as I'd never written anything before, but in those three weeks he gave me advice on how to get an agent, how to apply for a job, indeed he taught me the rudiments of how to begin a theatrical career – a debt I was never able to repay in full. I went back to Oldham. Luck again deserted Bill. His show, which was highly successful, was the last of its kind. The comedy, the wit, the humour, the point numbers were all being supplanted by a new post-war style of presentation, more robust, relics of the war, *Soldiers in Skirts*, *This Is The Show*, capital letters for each word (TITS) – obvious what the show was about. There were new comedians by the thousand, thankfully only a few gifted ones survived, but Bill's sophisticated approach, his subtle delivery, sadly was phased out. Stamina, talent, as for luck it can go and jump in the lake.

We last saw Bill in a television 'comedy' called *Bootsie and Snudge* in which Bill played the character of Snudge, a cretinous lout. It was a desecration of a super talent. Red Rum pulling a coal cart.

Life deals many a peculiar hand. Bill Fraser gave me a start in my career. Had it not been for him, I would have returned to the cotton mill and Bill would not have appeared in this book.

He died a long time ago and, if luck had anything to do with it, the day after his death would have been the day a lucrative contract from MGM might have been delivered to his house.

Thanks for everything Bill.

IRENE HANDL

In a class of her own…along with Kretzel and Pretzel

PROFILE

Born: 27 December 1901

Place of birth: London

Irene was the daughter of a Viennese banker and a French mother. When her mother died, Irene stayed at home to look after her father and consequently did not embark on an acting career until she was nearly forty.

Selected radio: *Hello Playmates, Doctor in the House*

Selected films: *Silent Dust* (1948), *The Belles of St Trinian's* (1954), *Brothers in Law* (1957), *I'm All Right, Jack* (1959), *The Rebel* (1961), *Heavens Above* (1963), *Morgan, A Suitable Case for Treatment* (1966), *Stand up Virgin Soldiers* (1977), *The Great Rock 'n' Roll Swindle* (1980), *Absolute Beginners* (1986)

Selected TV: *Hancock's Half-Hour* (1956-60), *Drake's Progress* (1957), *Educating Archie* (1958-59), *The Rag Trade* (1963), *Barney Is My Darling* (1965-66), *Mum's Boys* (1968), *For the Love of Ada* (1970-71), *Maggie and Her* (1978-79), *Metal Mickey* (1980-83), *Never Say Die* (1987)

Died: 29 November 1987

Our first office, Spike Milligan and myself, was five flights up from a greengrocer's shop. Five flights of uncarpeted stairs, a place of invention, inspiration and, in spite of the weather, the sun shone every day. There, Spike Milligan gave birth to *The Goon Show*, a noisy child that kept Spike up most nights. Our office in the sky, sounds of scratches from my pen and chuckles accompanying the tip tapping of the typewriter as Spike assaulted it with two fingers.

It was also a halfway house for celebrities who popped in any time they were passing and, as we were only a few hundred yards from the Lime Grove BBC Television studio, we naturally got their overflow.

We were usually glad to see them, flattered by the notoriety we were attracting, and the break in our routine was always welcome. Our favourite, however, was Irene Handl. We always knew when she was about to pay us a visit. The slow clomp of her feet on the uncarpeted stairs was the first intimation, followed by the harsh breathing when she came to a bend, slower clomping as she made her way up the next flight. Heavy breathing interrupted by muttered imprecations as she prepared herself for the final assault to the summit. Eventually, when she entered breathlessly, a Chihuahua under each arm, we adopted surprise and delight. 'How nice to see you, Irene.' Our delight was genuine and our surprise was not – from the third flight up we had written three pages of dialogue, the next hour would be Irene's.

We sat her in a chair, drew water for the Chihuahuas and a cup of tea for our guest. I sat on a corner of my desk; we only had two chairs. She always apologised saying, 'I hope I'm not interrupting your writing or anything.' We never found out what 'anything' implied but one thing was certain, we would be royally entertained for the next hour. She was a doll, a panacea for every ailment. First of all she took out two doggy bowls, put them on the floor and in each one placed a couple of pieces of cold chicken. She introduced her Chihuahuas, Kretzel and Pretzel. They say a dog's life is something to be shunned but Kretzel and Pretzel had got it made, cold chicken for lunch and they didn't even have to walk upstairs, all the time being fussed and fretted by Irene.

She was unique; there was no one like her and no one in her class of humour. Much of her idiosyncrasies were undoubtedly garnered from old theatrical landladies. For instance, when she was younger she was living in digs run by a harridan. When Irene, one mealtime, asked for the cruet, the landlady refused saying, 'If I give you a cruet they'll all want one.' On another occasion she was taking an old acquaintance to see her room but it was just after ten at night and one of the strict rules of the house was to the effect that young ladies were not allowed to bring male companions into their rooms after ten o'clock. Unfortunately, the dragon was standing at the foot of the stairs when they entered the vestibule.

'You're not taking him up to your room!' hissed the landlady. 'You know the rules.'

'He's an old friend of mine,' protested Irene.

'I don't care who he is,' she snarled, 'you're not turning my house into a Bovril.'

I can think of only one other actress with similar eccentricities as Irene, the inimitable Margaret Rutherford. The only difference being that Miss Rutherford strode down the street, mistress of all she surveyed, while Irene would enter her own home wondering if she was in the right place.

For the next thirty years or so Irene and I worked together in television and films, unfortunately never on stage. She appeared in more plays than most actors have had hot dinners and I'm surprised she hasn't been honoured with the Freedom of the City or at least the West End.

Another reason I would have liked to work in a stage play with Irene was to discover whether the following anecdote was fact or fiction. There are times when an actor in a play dries up, in other words, forgets his next line. There is usually a waffling and a fumbling to get back on track. Not so Irene. If she found herself in this situation she simply fainted. Gasp from the Front of House, curtains brought down followed by mutterings from the audience. Meanwhile, on stage, Irene would sit up and say, 'What is the flaming line?' and when she was quite certain where she was, the curtains opened and, if this anecdote is true, to tumultuous applause the play carried on, having created another legend to hang round Irene's neck.

Making films is normally a pleasurable experience for an actor, not so much for makeup with a large cast or wardrobe, as in Henry the Fourth Part Two, or even a harassed director when the money has dried up. Usually, though, a comedy film is a happier affair and as I've been mainly employed in this lighter side my favourite film was *Heavens Above* starring Peter Sellers as the hapless vicar who takes in a layabout family of skivers and work dodgers, with a little bit of petty pilfering to top up the dole, child benefits and whatever else was going in our glorious welfare state. I was the idle head of the feckless family, husband of Irene who in her turn had bred seven or eight scallywags. Irene was incredible. It wasn't so much what she said, it was the way she said it. During our scenes together I had to bust myself with something or other, or look somewhere because I knew if I'd caught sight of Irene I'd be gone – helpless with the giggles.

When Peter was addressing us all, as he was wont to do throughout the film, he ran into the same problem: he could not look at Irene. In the film, however, he was a jolly vicar and a few chuckles didn't come amiss.

In between takes Irene would toddle off to her caravan to feed or to pamper Kretzel and Pretzel, who couldn't possibly have been the originals when Irene used to visit our office, but I can just imagine her: 'There we are. Mummy wasn't long was she?' Why the little darlings had legs is beyond me, they were superfluous, she carried those dogs everywhere.

Irene appeared on one or two of our Eric and Hattie series, as well as in a few one-hour sketch shows of mine, and each time we worked together it was a joy. Incredibly, she looked just the same as she did when she made her frequent visits to entertain us in the early days, in spite of the stairs. I'll never know how she managed to negotiate the fruit and vegetables carrying Kretzel and Pretzel.

I can only assume that the greengrocer and his two assistants were exceedingly willing and happy to lift her over, touching their forelocks respectfully.

Sadly, our last television show together was one of my silent movies with Tommy Cooper and another two of my favourites, Richard Briers and Sylvia Sims. They should most certainly feature in this book but if I was to include all my Comedy Heroes it would take two sturdy librarians to lift it onto the shelf.

The silent movie was called *It's Your Move* and as it was a silent, Irene had nothing to say, which was sad in a way because half of Irene's attraction was her convoluted use of the English language. But just to see her was enough. After all, half of Irene is worth most of most aspiring comedians today.

With Irene's death, we have lost a funny, jolly, eccentric character and wherever she is now I hope and pray there will also be two look-alike Kretzels and Pretzels waiting to be carried around. Otherwise, dear Irene won't know what to do with her arms.

DICKIE HENDERSON

A gentleman in every respect

PROFILE

Born: 30 October 1922

Place of birth: London

The son of a vaudeville comic Dick Henderson, Dickie made his showbiz debut at the age of ten in the Hollywood version of Noel Coward's *Cavalcade*. He then appeared in variety with his sisters as The Henderson Twins and Dickie, but the act broke up when the twins married and the versatile Dickie went solo, achieving his TV break in Arthur Askey's *Before Your Very Eyes*.

Selected theatre: *Teahouse of the August Moon* (1955)

Selected TV: *Face the Music* (1953), *Before Your Very Eyes* (1953), *The Ed Sullivan Show* (1956), *Sunday Night at the London Palladium* (compere, 1958), *The Dickie Henderson Half-Hour* (1958-59), *The Dickie Henderson Show* (1960-68), *A Present for Dickie* (1969-70), *I'm Dickie – That's Showbusiness* (1978)

Died: 22 September 1985

Professionalism, personality, and above all style, those attributes would undoubtedly describe Dickie Henderson. Add to that charm, and as for talent, he carried it around by the sackful.

He was the most unassuming person I ever met which, unsurprisingly, was on a golf course. We were playing together in a pro-celebrity charity match and it was one of the most pleasurable days of my golfing career. He didn't try to dominate the proceedings with a series of comical reminiscences, although in later years I discovered he had a fund of stories about incidents that had happened to him in his life. He was born of a Vaudeville comic, Dickie Henderson Senior, his two sisters, The Henderson Twins, a very attractive pair, were also on the stage, but on that occasion of our first meeting it was difficult to accept he was brought up in a theatrical family.

On that golf day he was casually but impeccably dressed and although I'd heard of him, having been on the bill at the London Palladium with his father, so young Dickie was no stranger to me, after that eighteen holes of golf he was my role model. From that day I tried to emulate him. It lasted a week. It's too difficult to follow in the footsteps of someone who does everything so well with such panache and economy of movement . . .

He was a most modest person, slightly built, very rarely without a smile, in fact a person who would be successful in whatever profession or calling he put his mind to. Having said this, it is easy to understand why other comedians and entertainers placed him in the premier division.

Although from that first meeting we'd met again on several enjoyable occasions, it was a few years before I saw his act. As we are all so busy doing our own things up and down the country, indeed all over the world, we rarely get the chance or the luxury of watching other artistes on the stage, so it is not unusual. I believe I would have claimed him as one my 'Heroes' anyway, but after seeing him on the stage of the Palladium he became one of my 'Comedy Heroes'. Dickie was sensational, hilarious and it all seemed so effortless. His wasn't the suave, dinner jacket, black tie, raconteur approach, there were times during his act when he was extremely energetic.

Even now I smile at the recollection of Dickie, sitting on a high bar stool, doing a comedy routine in which he was singing à la Sinatra Set 'Em Up Joe. For those of you too young to remember, it depicted a maudlin drunk, sitting at the bar, three o'clock in the morning, confiding his troubles to a barman – hence the title Set 'Em Up Joe. It was hilarious as Dickie was, at the same time, desperately trying to knock a cigarette out of a pack with disastrous results.

In another of his acts, he played a hapless singer endeavouring to sing a popular number, hampered by the fact that he was holding his microphone attached to a long lead stretching into the wings. His antics on becoming entangled in the lead can't be described on paper; I could never do justice to something that had the audience out of control with laughter. This was only the tip of the iceberg, it wouldn't surprise me if he could ride a unicycle whilst juggling a set of Encyclopaedia Britannicas, and at the same time whistling the 'Marseillaise'.

With his pedigree it was natural that young Dickie Henderson was bitten by the theatre bug. He spoke fondly of his father – strict but not so much that Dickie's upbringing wasn't full of laughs. This was not always the case. Dickie told me once how in his early days on the stage he wasn't going down too well; in fact, poor

Dickie was dying a death. This was doubly unfortunate because his father was watching him from the wings. On the stage, the young Dickie was working his socks off to a mass of indifference. Sadly, his act was rapidly going down the plughole so, with the cockiness of youth, knowing his father was watching, Dickie came out with a load of old clichés to the audience – 'I know you're out there, I can hear you breathing' or 'Is the curtain up?' and other despairing lines trotted out by comedians from Cromwell's day. Finally, Dickie left the stage only to walk straight into a slap from his irate Father.

'What was that for?' he said, more puzzled than hurt.

His father replied, 'That's for telling them you were dying a death. If you hadn't come out with all that crap, "I can hear you breathing" and "Is the curtain up?" they'd have been none the wiser. They didn't know you were dying until you told them, they thought you were always that bad.'

When Dick told me that story he added a rider. 'It was a lesson I never forgot,' he said ruefully.

I never heard him speak ill of another and, on reflection, it seems to be obvious why. In the theatre there is a lot of gossip, backbiting, denigration, but all this is mainly amongst wannabes. When you are established there is no necessity for it and Dickie never did anything that was unnecessary.

Conversely, I never heard anyone make a derogatory remark about Dickie.

THORA HIRD

A delight to work with, a delight to talk with – a delightful lady

PROFILE

Born: 28 May 1911

Place of Birth: Morecambe, Lancashire

Thora made her acting debut at the age of just eight weeks in a play featuring her mother and directed by her father. She soon established herself as an accomplished young actress but kept her day job at the local Co-op where she studied her customers to use in future characterisations.

Selected films: *The Black Sheep of Whitehall* (1941), *Corridor of Mirrors* (1946), *The Weaker Sex* (1948), *Once a Jolly Swagman* (1948), *The Cure for Love* (1949), *One Good Turn* (1954), *Simon and Laura* (1955), *Sailor Beware* (1956), *The Entertainer* (1960), *A Kind of Loving* (1962), *The Nightcomers* (1971)

Selected TV: *Meet the Wife* (1964-66), *The First Lady* (1968-70), *Praise Be!* (1977-93), *In Loving Memory* (1979-86), *Intensive Care* (1982), *Hallelujah!* (1982-84), *Last of the Summer Wine* (1985-2003), *Cream Cracker Under the Settee* (1987), *Lost for Words* (1999)

Died: 15 March 2003

During the late fifties, I was writing and appearing in a series of television sketch shows, each week inviting a different star guest to join me in the frolics. I think it was a series of six and I am sure they all went down well. Well, I think they did. One thing I'll never forget: I wasn't asked to do a second series.

Nevertheless, one bright spot lights up my memory . . . my star guest, Thora Hird. It was a magic week of rehearsals with never a dull or ponderous moment. In fact, we spent more time swapping yarns than we did in learning the script, but then Thora was born in Morecambe and me in Oldham, so naturally we spoke the same language.

The producer of the series was my old friend Dennis Main Wilson and in our moments of reminiscing he would look from Thora's face to mine and back again, desperately trying to understand what we were saying. He couldn't decide whether or not to grant us asylum. He was reluctant to interrupt in case we were discussing the show, but he should have guessed – we laughed so much it couldn't possibly have anything to do with the script. If my memory serves me right, and it does quite often, I'm sure the show was successful, but for me, I'd found a new friend and, although I enjoyed working with all my other star guests, Thora was something else. Her genuine warmth and friendliness made the week extra special.

After the show she said to me, 'I'd love to do a summer season with you.' I shook my head.

'We'll work together again, Thora, but I don't do summer seasons.'

In fact, the thought of doing sixteen weeks in some stage production or other frightened the daylights out of me, but I desperately wanted to work with Thora again.

It was at that moment an idea began to take shape.

My first professional job in the theatre after the war had been at the Coliseum, Oldham, a Repertory Company of good reputation. I wasn't a regular member, I was only called upon when they needed a butler to say, 'You rang, my lady' or, if the extra part was written for a maid, I would be cast as the Manservant opening the door to admit real actors. Even so, I was getting three pounds a week when I worked but, more importantly, I was entitled to write 'actor' in my passport. Nevertheless, that was nearly ten years ago and I was now up with the ratings in television shows and far from answering doors and 'tea is served, your lordship' and rhubarb, rhubarb off.

I now owned a Bentley and the commissionaire at the BBC opened the door for me, so with this new elevated lifestyle, I said to Thora, 'Why don't you and I do a guest week at Oldham Rep?' Thora was delighted.

'I've been there once,' she said. 'I did a guest appearance a couple of months ago and it went well.'

I said, 'OK, Thora, I was with them ten years ago – leave it to me.'

And this is what happened . . .

I had my agent write to the Coliseum suggesting that Thora and I would be delighted to appear as guests for one week etc. etc. Three days later came the reply; they would indeed be delighted to welcome Miss Hird back again as she was such a huge success on her last visit. However, as for Eric Sykes, 'he's not really an actor, is he?'

I showed Thora the letter. She looked at me when she read the bit about not really being an actor, then we both burst out laughing. Getting her breath back, Thora said, 'I'm not really an actor either – only they didn't find me out.'

What a dear lady and a magnanimous way to treat the letter. She didn't get angry, she didn't offer sympathy and what's more important, she didn't ever appear at the Oldham Rep.

One of the people who knew Thora as well as anyone was Christopher Beeny. I know him well, having done pantomime with him twice at Windsor and a Stoppard play in Liverpool. More importantly, he had worked closely with Thora for six years in the television series called *In Loving Memory*. I didn't know Christopher at that time but I watched the show because whenever Thora appeared in whatever, I had to watch.

Having telephoned Christopher, he told me it was the happiest six years of his life and he related an anecdote from one of the shows. Apparently, in one scene, Christopher was having a bath in front of the fire, a common enough occurrence during the thirties when bathrooms were a luxury only the super-rich could afford. For most of the population, being the super-poor, they made do with a tin bath hanging from a nail in the backyard. I mention this because a bathroom today is as natural to a house as having a front door.

Back to *In Loving Memory* . . . Christopher is going through a normal Northern Friday night ritual of having a bath when there is a knocking at the front door and we hear the voice of Christopher's girlfriend.

'Hello' is there anybody in?'

Chris is panic stricken, leaps out of the bath and hides in the pantry. For obvious reasons, this could not be shown on television as this wasn't Channel 4, so to fill in while Chris runs to the pantry starkers, the director cuts to a shot of Christopher's girlfriend at the front door listening. When we cut back, the bath in front of the fire is empty. Thora then enters through the back door, sees the bath is uninhabited and assumes that Christopher is probably out on the town by now smelling like a carbolic factory so she opens the pantry door and lo and behold there stands a naked, panic-stricken Christoper holding a jelly mould in order to maintain some kind of modesty. Thora's line was, 'Why does it always happen to you?' End of show, or it should have been except the laughter from the audience was so loud and prolonged Thora's line was lost in the uproar, so naturally they had to retake the scene.

Again, on opening the pantry door the same reaction from the audience. Before retake three the Floor Manager was trotted out to ask the delighted audience to control their laughter. 'Otherwise we'll be here all night,' he added. More laughter. 'Action'. Thora opened the pantry door and this time the audience were more controlled but Thora wasn't . . . she started to giggle, pandemonium, again 'Cut'. Apologies from Thora to the dark glass hiding the producer and his staff, who most definitely wouldn't be enjoying the humour of the situation. In fact, after a few more takes it was getting to be hard work and Thora's line which was to end the show, 'Why does it always happen to you?' was now audible but repetition had diminished its humour.

Thora opened the pantry door, modest laughter and even the cowering, shivering Christopher holding the jelly mould to himself was beginning to lose interest but Thora, who hadn't earned her top-of-the-bill status for nothing, turned to the audience and said, 'My best jelly mould and all.' The audience roared, the music and the credits rolled.

My thanks to Christopher for sharing with me one of the joys of working with Thora in the series *In Loving Memory* and with the title of this show I can think of no more fitting tribute to our incomparable Thora.

FRANKIE HOWERD

The man who opened the door for me

PROFILE

Born: (Francis Alick Howard) 6 March 1917

Place of Birth: York

Determined to overcome a stammer and break into show-business, Frankie had resigned himself to working in an insurance office until war intervened and allowed him to hone his act. A series of troop shows alerted an agent and resulted in a successful audition for the popular radio show *Variety Bandbox*.

Selected radio: *Variety Bandbox* (1946-52), *Fine Goings On* (1951), *Frankie Howerd Goes East* (1952), *The Frankie Howerd Show* (1953-58), *Frankie's Bandbox* (1960), *Now Listen* (1964)

Selected theatre: *Pardon My French* (1953-54), *Charley's Aunt* (1955-56), *A Midsummer Night's Dream* (1957), *A Funny Thing Happened on the Way to the Forum* (1963)

Selected films: *The Runaway Bus* (1953), *The Ladykillers* (1955), *A Touch of the Sun* (1956), *Further up the Creek* (1958), *Watch It, Sailor!* (1961), *The Fast Lady* (1962), *The Great St Trinian's Train Robbery* (1965), *Carry On Doctor* (1967), *Up Pompeii!* (1970), *Up the Chastity Belt* (1971), *Up the Front* (1972), *The House in Nightmare Park* (1973)

Selected TV: *The Howerd Crowd* (1952), *Frankly Howerd* (1959), *Up Pompeii!* (1970), *Whoops Baghdad* (1973), *A Touch of the Casanovas* (1953), *All Change* (1989-91)

Died: 19 April 1992

After almost six years of World War II, one of the first big shows broadcasting every Sunday evening was *Variety Bandbox* produced by Joy Russell Smith and from the first day it was a roaring success.

Miss Russell Smith was unique in the BBC at that time. She obviously understood more about comedy than many of her contemporaries. The programme was exactly the tonic needed for a war-weary nation; it also gave ex-servicemen a flying start in their new careers. In fact, just being selected to do a six-minute spot on *Variety Bandbox* was the 'Open Sesame' to many theatrical agencies.

Every budding comedian would consider himself well on the way to top-of-the-bill status if he appeared on the show, especially if his or her act was new, fresh and original. Amongst this wealth of up-and-coming talent the brightest, most inspired, discovery by Miss Russell Smith was a young ex-soldier called Frank Howerd.

To be selected once to appear on *Variety Bandbox* was an accolade in itself, to appear twice was a real confidence booster. Frank was an instant hit and was given top spot in the programme, alternating with another new talent, Derek Roy. Eventually, Frank's popularity was such that he had an unbelievable audience rating of 42 per cent, almost half the population hanging on to his every word. Indeed, when Frank was on Britain was the quietest place in the world, apart from the Sahara. There were few cars on the road and a pedestrian was a rarity. Practically every homestead lucky enough to have a wireless set was tuned in to Frankie Howerd and those who did not possess a wireless knew friends who did. His impact was so great I firmly believe that if Frank had stood for parliament he might well have been our longest-serving Prime Minister. After a short time he dominated *Variety Bandbox* and before long he was doing three spots in the programme: an opening spot with Billy Ternent the resident bandleader, a middle spot with current popular film stars (and, believe me there was no shortage of candidates eager to appear with this amazing find), and finally Frank closed the show with his own act.

At that time I was a repertory actor in Warminster and, like millions of other devoted fans, my week's highlight was listening to the sheer brilliance of Frank's happy nonsense. Being a frustrated comedian, listening to Frank was like a penniless urchin looking into Hamley's shop window six days before Christmas. So you can imagine what a heart-stopping moment it was for me when Vic Gordon, one of my wartime comrades, telephoned and told me Frankie Howerd was trying to get in touch and would I call him on this number. Good grief! It was as if the King had contacted me for a game of skittles at Buckingham Palace. Almost before I'd put the telephone down I was dialling Frank's number. It's not easy dialling when you're floating three feet off the floor. I could hardly believe my ears when Frankie Howerd said, 'Hello.'

The next afternoon I was on the train to Sheffield where he was appearing in pantomime and as I approached the theatre, due to his enormous popularity, it appeared that most of the town had turned out in the hope of getting a ticket.

They shuffled forward, six deep, right round the theatre in spite of the fact that 'House Full' boards were displayed outside the box office – boards that, in all probability, hadn't been out since the 1930s – and it was only the matinee!

When I was shown into Frank's dressing room he was getting ready for the show. He looked different from what I had imagined. I don't think I had ever bothered my head about what he looked like but when he spoke I knew immediately I was in the right place. During the course of our conversation he explained that radio was a voracious animal eating up material every Sunday and would I write for him?

Apart from his summons, this was the second biggest shock as I'd never written a script in my life. In any case, my mouth was quicker than my brain, 'Whew,' it said. 'When do you want to start?' and before the matinee was over I'd written Frank's first script. It wasn't about jokes, it was a situation, i.e. Frank's first job as a messenger boy was to take two elephants to Crewe. I wrote it as if Frank was delivering, using 'Ooh . . . Ah . . . No . . . Listen . . . No, Listen . . .' as punctuation marks, as did Frank. I read it to him in a passable impersonation of his own voice and he was delighted with it, and I was a scriptwriter.

Incidentally, to clear up the mystery of why he contacted me in the first place, it was sheer coincidence. When the war ended I was in Schleswig-Holstein, along with thousands of other servicemen at a loose end just waiting out our time for demob. During this period I volunteered to take part in a revue. Most of us were amateurs, one of the exceptions being Flight Lieutenant Bill Fraser, and from there I was transferred to Army Welfare Services, becoming principal comedian in a revue called *Strictly Off The Record*. The Army Welfare Services put out other shows, one being *The Waggoners*. The principal comedian was Frankie Howerd. We never met in Germany but when Frank was flying high in *Variety Bandbox* he remembered 'that other comedian' and his reason for getting in touch was to buy my act.

Frank was a great inspiration to me. Over the years I discovered what an amazing person he really was. An avid reader of philosophy, science and most of the great writers, his only light reading was novels by Agatha Christie. He thoroughly enjoyed his visits to the Albert Hall and Wigmore Hall to listen to Orchestral concerts. He was an excellent tennis player; indeed, his pleasures were totally at odds with his 'Ooh-Ah-No-Listen' persona on stage. Like many great comedians he was implacably at odds with his comedy character. His real heartfelt ambition was to have been a straight actor, preferably Shakespeare or Chekhov, etc. In fact, he failed an audition for RADA, his first attempt at theatre on being demobbed. Thank God he didn't make it. We wouldn't have had one of our greatest comedians and Hamlet would be getting laughs!

After his extraordinary success in *Variety Bandbox* he attracted agents like sharks in a feeding frenzy. Unfortunately, it seemed to me, that most agencies at that time treated radio with a wary suspicion that it wouldn't last. There were many good, established agencies in practice at that time, however, so how Frank got involved with Jack Payne will always remain a mystery. Jack Payne was a band leader and had he paid more attention to his music, and less to managing Frank, his records might still be available.

For instance, he booked Frank to appear in a revue called *Tar-Ra-Ra-Boom Deay* – not a very inspired title but the show was good. It was the biggest theatrical event of the year. It toured with an enormous cast including its own orchestra – one of the most extravagant spectacles since records were kept and, incredibly, Frankie Howerd was not top of the bill. He was undoubtedly the star of the show but another act, Jean Adrienne and Eddie Leslie, closed the show.

Inevitably, it was a smash hit and Dean Moray, the impresario, deservedly raked in enough to keep his bank manager smiling for years. The show was such a hit they naturally decided to stage a follow-up entitled *Tar-Ra-Ra-Booms Again* and, as I'd written all the comedy for the original, I was asked to write this one, too.

After scripting most of it I was dumbstruck, astounded, aghast. In fact, I didn't believe it at first but the sad truth was Jack Payne believed that Jean and Eddie were the stars of the show and Frankie Howerd, his own client mind you, was just a flash in the fryer! Frank wasn't even in the production – he'd been replaced by an old comic, Leon Cortez. Good, reliable and steady but hardly in the same league as Frank.

Tar-Ra-Ra-Booms Again limped out on tour and the limp became more pronounced until, after a few weeks, crutches wouldn't have helped and sadly all the gains made by Dean Moray were wiped out, and then some. But the real tragedy was Frank. Being extremely sensitive, he had been knocked sideways. He could accept not being top-of-the-bill in his first touring show, but in the second tour, to be dropped altogether was devastating.

Shortly afterwards Frank left Jack Payne, who was blissfully unaware of the gold nugget that had slipped through his fingers. Frank lost confidence, became morose, and was now enjoying large gin and tonics. Johnny Speight, another writer and, in my opinion, one of our greatest comedy writers, was a great admirer of Frank's talent and suggested that something had to be done. One evening in my office, Johnny, Simpson and Galton and myself sat Frank down in a chair and, after four hours of hard grind, we'd concocted a script for him.

Frank was delighted and when he went on television with his new-found material, so was everyone who knew him. He was back on top again, Frankie Howerd was reborn. He next appeared at a club run by Peter Cook and, if confirmation was needed, he took the place by storm.

In my opinion he was too big a personality to shine in television and unsure of himself in films. On radio he was supreme but his true medium was the stage. To watch him breathe life into a listless audience and, in less than five minutes, hold them in the palm of his hand as they rocked and laughed themselves helpless was a privilege. His vocal range was incredible, from a low growl to an old church door opening, his expensive suits were made to measure, but sadly failed to fit.

My everlasting thanks to you, Frank, for opening up the very first door of my career and thanks again for shoving me through it.

HATTIE JACQUES

My identical twin sister

PROFILES

Born: 7 February 1924

Place of Birth: Sandgate, Kent

Hattie trained as a hairdresser but worked as a nurse and an arc welder in a London factory during WWII. Her showbiz career began on stage at the Little Players Theatre after the war.

Selected radio: *ITMA, Educating Archie, Hancock's Half Hour*

Selected films: *Green for Danger* (1946), *Oliver Twist* (1948), *A Christmas Carol* (1951), *Old Mother Riley Meets the Vampire* (1952), *The Love Lottery* (1954), *Carry on Sergeant* (1958), *School for Scoundrels* (1960), *Carry On Cabbie* (1963), *The Plank* (1967), *Carry On Camping* (1969), *Carry On Matron* (1973), *Carry on Dick* (1975)

Selected TV: *Sykes, Our House, Miss Adventure, Rhubarb, Rhubarb, That Was the Week That Was*

Died: 6 October 1980

No words of mine will adequately express my depth of feeling for my dear friend, Hattie. How much I miss her; she brought sunshine to the darkest day and when she was around troubles went somewhere else and laughter was never more than a twinkle away.

In the late forties I was invited to see a show at The Players' Theatre, underneath the arches in Villiers Street. I was flattered, at least somebody thought I was somebody. I had no idea what the show was about, it could have been ballet or *King Lear* on ice for all I cared. In the event I was in for a pleasant surprise and more importantly, it was to be the turning point in my life.

The Players' Theatre is unique; it is a Music Hall in a time warp. Toast Master was on the side of the stage banging his gavel on the table as he introduced the acts, all dressed in the costumes of the late nineteenth century. We, the audience, sat at round tables, pints of beer for the men, champagne for the ladies and for the honoured guest, a large malt whisky, which I didn't really need – I was already intoxicated by the atmosphere. Cigarette and cigar smoke warmed the auditorium and I was feeling that this night was going to be special.

Bang went the gavel and we all stood and raised our glasses, we drank to the health of Queen Victoria and the show commenced. We all joined in the choruses of the popular old tunes, laughed at the popular old jokes and between acts we were all on our feet cheering when the Toast Master announced the relief of Mafeking. We drank to our soldiers in Africa. It was a wonderful, proud moment.

With several bangings of the gavel the Toast Master brought the house to order as he announced the next act with an extremely flowery build-up. He ended with rising voice, 'I give you, your own, your very own, Miss

Hattie Jacques!' Again, pandemonium, whistles and cheers. Whoever this 'Miss Hattie Jacques' was, she had the audience with her. In fact, her reception put the relief of Mafeking in its place.

On to the stage exploded a jolly, buxom, young lady as cockney as Bow Bells, smile that outshone the footlights and with a large bird cage in her hand. She captured the audience with the favourite 'My Old Man Said Follow The Van And Don't Dilly Dally On The Way'. She moved about the stage with an elegance and grace as if she owned it. At the end of her act, to great applause, she leapt in the air, finishing in the splits, landing as softly as a snowflake in July. I knew for a certainty here was a young lady with a future ahead.

Coincidentally, a new comedy half hour was about to take to the air on radio. *Educating Archie* was written by myself and Sid Colin, a fellow scriptwriter owed so much by so many. Peter Brough, a ventriloquist, and his dummy Archie Andrews, were to be the stars and, apart from a very young Julie Andrews, it was an all male cast. That was before I'd been to The Players' Theatre and when the show was launched a new name was added, Hattie Jacques.

The show was an instant success. Peter Brough was delighted, the BBC astonished and, unbeknown to me at the time, I'd found my identical twin sister, Hat.

After the radio show a new medium, television, was growing like a fungus. Pictures in homes . . . it was a staggering advance on what was becoming known as steam radio.

In these early days of television, when the pictures were in black and white, cameramen, dressers and makeup were mainly recruited from film studios and the stagehands from the theatre. All were experienced.

The unknown factor was the newly fashioned sitcom and, even more unknown were the producers, making the almost impossible leap from radio to television with only a six-month course learning to 'track in and track out', although they had no idea of what to 'track in and track out' to, so the onus was most definitely on the performers.

We were one of the luckier shows, we had Hattie Jacques, and if that wasn't enough, there was Richard Wattis and Deryck Guyler, two very experienced comedy actors in films, radio and theatre. Being the writer I was able to script most of the lines for Hattie, Richard and Deryck. My own lines were 'What?', 'Who did?', 'When?' etc. I'm no fool; why pick up a bucket of water when the fire-brigade is right behind you?

Hattie was brilliant and went through each performance as if she'd known that television was about to be invented, as if she'd known that she was learning her craft in preparation for its inception. Whatever I wrote she delivered as if it had been scripted by George Bernard Shaw and if a line was really appalling she would suggest another one – strangely exactly the one I would have written had I thought about if first.

I believe it was mainly due to Hat's personality on the screen that the BBC reluctantly asked if we'd do another series. We were overjoyed and accepted immediately and after that second series they reluctantly asked us if we would do another one. In fact they were still asking us reluctantly twenty years later!

However, in the early, tentative years of television there were no such safeguards as retakes, cuts or dubbed laughter. If the audience didn't laugh, too bad, that was it, we were live.

Our show was at 8.30 to 9 o'clock. It had to be written and

performed to the exact second. If the show wasn't finished at the appointed time a dinner-jacketed announcer would appear on the screen saying, 'Good evening, this is the nine o'clock news.' Indeed, some viewers must have thought he was part of our show. As writer, I had a very difficult balancing job to do. For instance, if it was an exceptionally good audience, we'd be getting more laughs in which case, with still two or three minutes of our show to run, up popped 'Good evening, this is the nine o'clock news.' So then we had to invent some way of letting the cast know whether we were running late or with time in hand, ergo the floor manager, in contact with the producer via his ear-phones, would stretch his arms out wide meaning we had time in hand and if he whirled his hand round like cranking an old motor car, it meant, 'Get your skates on.' His antics were reminiscent of a batsman guiding down a jet fighter onto the deck of an aircraft carrier. With growing confidence, his signals became more flamboyant and in some cases got as many laughs as the show itself.

All this will, I hope, give you some idea of the un-charted waters we had to navigate in the early days but I'd like to highlight one of the many reasons why the series ran for twenty years. Dear old Hat.

As we were 'live' in those days the writing style encountered more hazards. If, for instance, one scene ended with us going upstairs to bed, then immediately it was the following day. It was a perilous situation and the following actually happened.

Hat went upstairs to bed saying, 'Good night, Eric. See you in the morning.' Then, as she disappeared through the door at the top of the stairs, she stepped on to a raised platform where a dresser was waiting to change her into her morning costume. In the meantime, I was left downstairs moaning about why it was always me who had to lock up, when the floor manager signalled that Hattie was ready. I said, 'I'll have to do the boiler as well,' ducking through a small door leading presumably to the cellar. As I did so, Hat came down the stairs in a different dress. Over her shoulder she shouted, 'Breakfast in ten minutes, Eric,' and then she drew open the curtains. Daylight flooded in, a new day. How did they manage that? But congratulations were premature.

Round the back I was now in my pyjamas and dressing gown, I rushed to the ladder from where I was to climb up to the platform then appear through the door, yawning as I went downstairs. That's what should have happened. However, there was one little snag – a helluva big one actually. There was no ladder. When the dresser had finished Hattie and climbed down, a stage hand had taken the ladder away to some place unknown. Even the stage hand couldn't be found and the platform was out of my reach.

On stage, Hat, realising something was wrong, was brilliant. To fill the time she fed the goldfish, asking them had they slept well. She picked up a newspaper off the mat, read out the headlines upstairs to me as if it was all part of the show. The headlines came from her own fertile brain: 'Boer War Imminent.' Then, almost to herself, she said, 'I must change our newsagent.'

Meanwhile, round the back it was silent panic. If I didn't get on soon we'd have 'Good evening, this is the nine o'clock news.' There was only one thing for it. I rang the doorbell and when Hat let me in I entered in pyjamas and dressing gown and quick as a flash Hat said, 'Oh, Eric, you've been sleep-walking again!' It was the biggest laugh in the show and before we could carry on the dinner-jacketed announcer appeared . . . and even he was smiling.

Dear, unflappable, adaptable Hat.

In between series Hattie and I very rarely met or even telephoned each other. Hat would appear in films and when she was not working her home was open house to actors, actresses or even anybody in the street looking miserable and in need of a good hot meal. Richard Wattis and Deryck Guyler had time to do whatever they fancied. For myself, I had to write the next series and when we assembled for the first day of rehearsal it was a family reunion after long absences, swapping happy reminiscences of happenings since our last get together. It was as if we had taken off from a dark, cold Heathrow to break through the glowering clouds into a clean blue sky lit by a smiling sun. For the next couple of months we lived in our family home of Sebastopol Terrace on television but, like the good soul she was, Hattie invited millions of viewers to join us.

JIMMY JAMES

Last of the vaudevillians

PROFILE

Born: (James Casey) 1892

Place of birth: Stockton-on-Tees

Jimmy began as a juvenile performer, 'Terry-the-Blue-eyed Irish Boy', but after being gassed in the First World War, he was unable to sing again and so turned to comedy. His most famous routine was as a drunk ... even though he didn't touch alcohol in real life.

At the height of his fame he was chosen to appear in the Royal Variety Show of 1953, the year of the coronation.

Selected theatre: *Nights at the Comedy* (1964)

Selected TV: *Don't Spare the Horses* (1952), *Christmas Box* (1955), *Home James* (1956), *Meet the Champ* (1960)

Died: 4 August 1965

If you are under fifty years of age you may have heard the name Jimmy James but it is highly unlikely you will have seen him on stage.

Jimmy James was probably one of the last of the Vaude-villians but that isn't why I bring him to these pages; he's here simply because he made me laugh. In fact, he had the same effect on anyone who watched him.

Why were these old comics so good, so polished, their timing impeccable and why may we not see their great-ness today? In this twenty-first century we have other distractions – television, radio, clubs, pubs, wall to wall football, more money, more time for recreation and, worst of all, it is now mandatory to possess a sense of humour, even in straight debates on television, radio and even parliament. The participants seize on any opportu-nity to butt in with a quip or a funny line and one funny line begets another and aren't we witty, jolly people? So today why bother to devote your life to something that everybody seems to be doing already?

Back to Jimmy James and the old Vaudeville. To them it wasn't just an occupation, it was a vocation in a profes-sion harder to join than a Masonic Lodge. It is possible that Jimmy James, amongst other hopefuls in the late nineteenth century, would have started his career as a second spot comic – a thankless task as audiences only attended the theatres in order to see the main attraction. Every performance, if he was allowed, it was customary for the keen, eager hopeful to watch and learn from whoever was top-of-the-bill. This is a slow learning curve and even approaching the end of a long illustrious career most comics are still figuring out ways to improve; being a funny man doesn't necessarily make you a comic. You still have to convince the paying public.

Nowadays, through the medium of television, it is

possible to attain the high pedestal of 'stardom' by the time one is twenty-five, but then the real work begins, i.e. staying there – a daunting task for a twenty-five-year-old star with forty-odd years to maintain top-of-the-line status.

However, between two World Wars the young Jimmy James would have been happy in his work. In fact, anybody in the lean years in the North East would be happy to be in work and if not happy, at least better off than most.

To those who have never seen Jimmy on stage I can only say you missed a treat. He would walk on in a crumpled suit, collar and tie, trilby and a lighted cigarette, dragging away on it then puffing the smoke out of both sides of his mouth like a leaking steam locomotive. He would regale the audiences with a few anecdotes from a very old, lived-in face, for all the world looking like the morning after a reunion. He appeared to be an alcoholic desperately trying to convince anyone within earshot that he hadn't had a drop since breakfast, but this was only his stage persona because in real life Jimmy was a staunch teetotaller. After a few minutes of banter in his act he would be interrupted by a very long, wall-eyed idiot in a top coat down to his ankles, his opening line to Jimmy was, ''Ere, is it you that's putting it around that I'm barmy?'

This part was played for many years by an actor called Bretton Woods, or perhaps that was only his stage name. It was a joy to see Jimmy's puzzled expression looking off stage and into the audience. Finally he replied, 'No, but if you find out who it is you've got him.'

After more word fencing with this stuttering refugee from the asylum they would be interrupted by another implausible character carrying a small box, it could have been a shoe box, under his arm going by the unlikely name of Hutton Conyers. Jimmy was now in the middle, puffing nervously on his cigarette as he enquired, 'What's in the box?' to which Hutton told him he was on a trip up the Zambezi where he met the Chief of the Unganonga tribe and the Chief, being so taken by this white-faced visitor, presented him on his departure with a fully grown lion.

Jimmy asked, 'Where is it?' and Hutton replied, 'It's in the box.' Jimmy turned to the tall, cadaverous one on his right and winked as if to signify, 'We've got a right one here.' Then, light-heartedly playing him like a fish he said, 'Oh, yes, that was very nice of him.' Bretton nodded and replied, 'He presented me with a giraffe as well.'

Jimmy's eyebrows would shoot up into his hairline.

'Where is it?' he asked. Both he and Bretton pointed and together said, 'It's in the box.' During the next few minutes he told Jimmy of many more presents he'd received until by the end he had more animals in the box than at Whipsnade. It sounds implausible but take it from me it was hilarious nonsense.

My recollections of their act are dredged up from my memory bank. As the last time I saw him was over fifty years ago, the words they say may not be strictly accurate but I hope you get the picture.

It is the little things that linger in my mind. For instance, in one of his sketches he had a row with his wife. He decides to end it all. He puts a noose round his neck slinging the other end of the rope over a beam. Everything ready, he stands on a chair which wobbles. Quickly, Jim steps down, murmuring, 'That's not safe.'

In another sketch, Jimmy is in white tie and tails, top hat, clutching a half empty bottle of whisky, obviously two sheets to the wind. It is late at night, along comes a policeman and after the obligatory 'Hello, hello, hello' he says, 'You're out late.'

Jimmy, bleary eyed, suddenly recognises the policeman. 'Wait a minute,' he hiccups. 'Aren't you Ginger Dunne?'

The policeman says, 'That's right.'

Jimmy then replies, 'I thought I recognised you. You were the water-cart corporal.'

Soon they are sitting side by side exchanging reminiscences of the war, Jim passes over the bottle and the policeman says, 'Cheers' and starts to glug while Jimmy looks on as the level of the Scotch goes down.

Taking the bottle from his lips in order to breathe, the policeman looks at Jimmy and says, 'Where's yours?' to which Jimmy replies, 'It's under yours if I can get at it.'

Why were these old time comedians so good? I'll explain. In the early days of Jimmy's career the comedians usually only possessed two acts because it was possible in those days to tour the provinces for one year with act number one, then to tour the next year with act number two, and the year after back to number one again. Usually the contracts would include a clause 'Act as known' but there was nothing to stop the same act being improved. Most of the top liners not only improved but made their 'act as known' topically acceptable so that by the time they played a theatre their act, although basically the same, would be developed into a masterpiece of entertainment.

A producer from television asked me, 'Could you write a series for Jimmy James?' to which I replied, 'I don't know until we've spoken to each other.' Secretly, I was thrilled. It was a golden opportunity to meet one of my idols. Subsequently, I went to see Jimmy when he was appearing at the Empire Theatre, Oldham. I was shown into his dressing room full of trepidation – me, not the dressing room – but I need not have worried. He bade me to sit down, then apologised that he'd got no booze in the place, but I was welcome to a cup of tea. I nodded and he shouted into a little alcove, 'Make that two!'

'Have you come far?' he said.

'No,' I said. 'This is my home town, just visiting the old folks.'

'I come from the North East,' he said.

'I know,' I replied.

The conversation wasn't scintillating but it filled in time until the tea was served. It was brought in by a man about as old as Jimmy, struggling with two steaming mugs in one hand whilst manipulating a crutch under his other arm to keep his balance. He slopped down the tea in front of Jimmy, blowing on his fingers as he hippity-hopped back into his alcove.

When he'd gone, Jimmy said, 'He's only got one leg.'

Automatically, I said, 'I'm sorry.'

'Don't worry,' said Jimmy, 'he knows about it. He's looked after me for years.'

I nodded. 'It's his right leg that's missing,' and Jimmy beckoned me closer so as not to be overheard.

'He has a mate who's lost his left leg.'

'Oh, yes,' I said, as if I was interested. Jimmy went on, 'And every year on July the second they travel to Leicester together and buy a pair of shoes.'

For years I could imagine them both on the train to Leicester deciding whether to go for brogues or maybe brown suede.

Anyway, I didn't write the series for Jimmy. He said he'd always admired my work but his son, Cass, was a budding writer at that time, and Jimmy wanted to give him a chance. Of course, I understood and Jimmy James went higher in my esteem. Is it any wonder he was one of my first choices in my book of admiration?

BUSTER KEATON

Genius of the silent screen

PROFILE

Born: (Joseph Francis Keaton) 4
October 1895

Place of Birth: Piqua, Kansas

After performing in vaudeville
with his parents as The Three
Keatons, Buster became in-
trigued by the new motion picture
industry and was taken under the
sizeable wing of silent movie star
Roscoe 'Fatty' Arbuckle before
striking out on
his own.

Selected films: *One Week* (1920),
The Playhouse (1922), *The Boat*
(1922), *The Paleface* (1922),
Cops (1922), *Our Hospitality*
(1923), *The Navigator* (1924),
The General (1927), *Steamboat
Bill Junior* (1927), *The Camera-
man* (1928), *San Diego I Love
You* (1944), *Railrodder* (1965)

Selected TV: *The Buster Keaton
Show* (1950), *The Man Who
Bought Paradise* (1965)

Died: 1 February 1966

A number of readers will turn to this page and, if you're under sixty years of age, you can be forgiven for saying, 'Who the dickens was Buster Keaton?' For a start, he was my first boyhood Comedy Hero, years before Laurel and Hardy joined him in my happy memories.

When I was just a lad in the early thirties, I would save up for weeks until I had a penny, which was the price of admission at my local cinema, the Imperial, where I first discovered Buster Keaton. Once seated in the flickering darkness I would be mesmerised by his antics. These were the early days of filming, black and white, soundless and, in our case, accompanied by an elderly lady pianist in the pit, who watched the action on the screen and busked accordingly – a rousing few bars when the US Cavalry arrived and a softer touch when the lovers met. Most of this, however, was drowned in the boos and hisses that came from the audience and if the lover had had a kiss there'd be whistles and the lady pianist would glare furiously at us over the pit rail. In later years, however, at the Gaumont cinema in the town centre the lights would come up and, rising from the pit, an organist at the mighty Wurlitzer would play a series of popular melodies of the day. He was a portly man in white tie and tails, smiling over his shoulder now and again while most of us were fascinated by the shape of his corset underneath his tailcoat.

How the mind wanders . . . let me play back the years to the Imperial again and the halcyon days of Buster Keaton and the lady pianist. We never saw a film in its entirety, frequently the reels broke and the picture would either freeze or whizz through until the end of the film. The house lights would go up and it was then the custom for the audience to throw orange peel, apple cores, or whatever came to hand at the screen, the cinema echoing with derisive whistles until the manager walked onto the stage and shouted, 'You can pack that in' and what's more we did. It was the age when we obeyed any command from an official or someone in higher authority. After explaining the fault which was being rectified he marched off the stage and we sat quietly with bowed heads as a minion would enter with a broom to clear up the debris. Eventually, after a short wait, the house lights would go down and Buster would be with us again, sometimes upside down – another short wait.

I'm not sure if he starred in any of those movies but he always played a prominent part, dodging on and off horse-drawn trams, being chased by Keystone Cops, whatever the scene was he outshined. He was a trained acrobat doing impossible stunts with a deadpan expression any professional poker player would give a Royal Flush to possess.

Being unable to find any documentation on Buster Keaton, I had an inspiration: an old acquaintance of mine, Dick Lester, an American film director. I got to know Dick when he arrived in England and his first directing assignment was a short silent film with the unlikely title of Standing, Running and Jumping starring Spike Milligan and Peter Sellers to name but several. I didn't appear but contributed to the non-existent script. More importantly to me, Dick had worked with Buster Keaton and, although Buster was approaching the 'big sleep', he was still making films. Dick, like me, was a great fan of Keaton's when Buster was at the top and working on all cylinders. He broke every bone in his body by insisting on doing all his own stunts; he was a superb mime artist, all these qualities that are a rarity today. Due to the stampede to reach the finishing line we seem to have lost the patience, or the determination to learn basic crafts

. . . I only hope and pray that, in years to come, archive footage of the early Buster Keaton will be discovered, by which time perhaps we'll have the technology to update them for all to see and enjoy.

LAUREL & HARDY

Two gentle souls who taught me how to laugh

PROFILE

Stan Laurel
Born: (Arthur Stanley Jefferson)
16 June 1890

Place of Birth: Ulverston, Lancashire (now Cumbria)

Oliver Hardy
Born: 18 June 1892

Place of Birth: Harlem, Georgia

A music hall comic in England, Stan emigrated to the US in 1910 where he resumed his career in vaudeville. He made his film debut in 1918 and while working for producer Hal Roach, met Oliver 'Babe' Hardy, a cinema owner who had taken up acting.

Selected films: *The Battle of the Century* (1927), *Two Tars* (1928), *Big Business* (1929), *The Perfect Day* (1929), *Hog Wild* (1930), *Laughing Gravy* (1931), *Helpmates* (1931), *Dirty Work* (1933), *Them Thar Hills* (1934), *Tit for Tat* (1935), *Way Out West* (1936), *Blockheads* (1938), *A Chump at Oxford* (1940)

Stan Laurel died: 23 February 1965

Oliver Hardy died: 7 August 1957

Two of my earliest Comedy Heroes were Laurel and Hardy. I was only three years old when they formed their partnership in 1926, so by the time I was old enough to see them in the cinema they were a well-established comedy duo.

Going to the pictures before World War II was a very special treat for me, from the silent films to the talkies, to Stan Laurel and Oliver Hardy. When their introductory music chirped merrily from the loud speakers, a stir of happy expectation rustled through the audience. In my opinion Stan and Ollie leave all other comedy duos at the starting gate while they are at the two furlong marker. They didn't rely on smart lines; in fact they didn't even rely on the written word; they were absolutely, and deliciously, visual. To see them walk down a street gave one a glow of eager anticipation. It was funny, warm, full of the joys, striding out on a stroll that inevitably led to disaster.

Possibly the ground rules appertaining to filmmaking had not yet been written, which is just as well because Stan and Ollie would have walked right over them. For example, it was the norm for comedians to be terrorised by a huge brute of a man. To me the predictable outcome was always victory for the underdog, a deliberate attempt to manufacture pathos, as in Chaplin films. Stan and Ollie, however, were petrified by a diminutive little Scotsman who barely reached Ollie's shoulder, and there was genuine pathos, a quality I've always maintained you either have or you haven't got – these two possessed more than their fair share.

Chaplin, in my opinion, was successful only because he was one of the first screen comedians. His films were shot at sixteen frames a second, or under cranked, in other words, he had only to sit on a chair and cross his legs, which at speed became an almost acrobatic feat. In fact, all films of that era had the growing pains of doubling the normal speed of action. This helps the fun, but it is embarrassing when it is a documentary of perhaps the funeral of the Archduke Ferdinand. Any serious occasion becomes comic – enough said.

Rule 2 – do not look directly into the camera. Well, pardon me but that is exactly what Ollie did. In fact, half of Ollie's humour was based on bringing the viewing audience into his confidence. Never, ever did he speak to them, but his look was enough.

In one of their films, he watched Stanley completely absorbed in filling his palm with tobacco. Ollie's look signified, 'What's he doing now?' Stan clenched his fist over the tobacco, bringing his outstretched thumb to his mouth, a couple of experimental puffs on his thumb, satisfied that it was drawing well. He flicked the thumb on his other hand and a flame shot up. He applied this to the tobacco and when he exhaled smoke into the air he blew out the flame on his thumb. Not a word passed between them and after a puzzled look into the lens, Ollie surreptitiously began flicking his thumb, naturally without success. Through the film Ollie, getting more exasperated by the minute, was constantly flicking his thumb to no avail and only at the end of the film was he successful when a gout of flame shot from his thumb. His panic-stricken gyrations in his effort to put the fire out ended the film on a high note.

A further rule applied in filmmaking says 'do nothing abstract'. Well, if pipe smoking from your hand is not abstract, I've completely misunderstood the word. So much for regulations!

One of their most endearing qualities was their old world courtesy: raising their hats for ladies, opening doors for ladies, giving up their seats for ladies. Ollie, the experienced man of the world, flicking his tie with delicate coyness, nudging Stan to raise his hat, observing all the niceties of protocol already declining in the civilised Western World. In fact, they respected and revered all ladies with the exceptions of the ones they happened to be married to at the time, strong and ferocious, dominating Stan and Ollie in spite of their hollow attempts at being the masters.

Not every film they made was a hotshot at the box office but even the less hilarious adventures of Laurel and Hardy were a tonic in the hard, hungry thirties, and I honestly believe they were not fully aware of the magnitude of their international following.

During the making of a film on the beach at Barrow-in-Furness, I had a day off. In other words, I wasn't in the schedule for the next day's shooting. 'Great,' I thought and then I looked round me at the limitless vista of sand dunes . . . scrub . . . a bleak desolate wasteland . . . in the opposite direction, miles away across the water, the derelict silhouettes of the huge cranes watching over the remains of a dead shipbuilding industry. One thing was sure, I wasn't going to spend my precious day off here. I craved for human habitation: houses, pubs, anywhere that didn't remind me of the end of the world. Then, my head down in thought, I spotted a diamond. Ulverston, the birth place of my hero Stan Laurel was only a short distance away. He wouldn't be there now, of course, but at least I could walk the same streets he had trod almost a hundred years ago.

It is a delightful town and I felt not much had changed since when Stanley Jefferson lived there, played and dreamed of becoming Stan Laurel. Staring around me as if I was from another planet, I was jerked out of my

ABOVE
In *Big Bad Mouse*, Jimmy Edwards had to drink cold tea made to look like whisky, so this settles the score...

LEFT
Big Bad Mouse started off as a disaster but became a huge success and a great way for two old friends to carry on working together.

ABOVE
Warren Mitchell, Jimmy,
the author, Reg Varney and
Dick Emery share a joke at
the expense of the press
cameras.

BELOW
This publicity shot from
early in Irene Handl's career
contrasts starkly with...

BELOW
...this photo of her in the
1980s TV series *Metal
Mickey*.

ABOVE
With Hattie Jacques. The pose is for the camera but the smiles and the affection are entirely genuine.

LEFT
With a very glamorous Hattie.

ABOVE
Hattie was an immeasurable asset to any TV show.

LEFT
Spike Milligan.

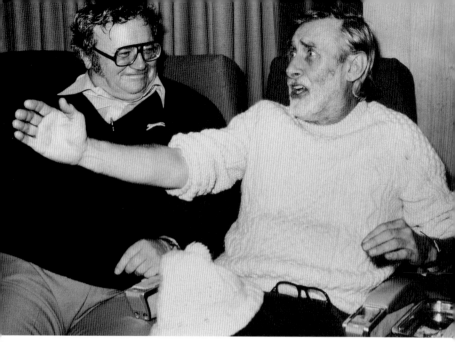

With Johnny Speight.
We were firm friends
from the very first
meeting.

Wilson, Keppel and
Betty on the bill at the
London Palladium and
during their famous
sand dance routine.

ABOVE
Although his voice became one of the most listened to on radio. Frankie Howerd's audience didn't really know what he looked like.

LEFT
Rob Wilton at his desk.

reveries when a little old man said, 'You'll be wanting the museum' and before I could ask, 'What museum?' he took my arm gently and led me across the road and down a side street, smiling up at me all the time.

Passers-by must have thought he was some sort of official, humouring and returning an escapee to the asylum. However, in a few more minutes we stopped outside a little open door leading to a dark interior. 'That's what you want isn't it?' and he even touched his cap and disappeared. How on earth did he know that this was exactly what I wanted? It was a shrine to Laurel and Hardy. I felt as if I was on consecrated ground . . . the first man to enter the pyramid of Tutankhamun . . . all about me were relics and memorabilia appertaining to the pair, old grained photographs of Stan through his years before he teamed up with Oliver Hardy. Naturally, the accent was on the local lad, Stan Laurel.

The shop owner, or possibly the curator, welcomed me and took me on a guided tour. Although there hadn't been many locals out in the street there were plenty of people in here, in another room continuous films of Laurel and Hardy were being shown in never-ending succession.

I asked the curator if he got any visitors from overseas and immediately a loud voice behind me boomed, 'Ja, I am from Hamburg.' He was a large German and couldn't have been more than forty years old. Apparently, hardly a day goes by without some visitors to this Mecca of adoration. For many of them, I can imagine the surprised expression of disbelief at the humble, down-to-earth establishment honouring the memory of two of the best-loved entertainers in the world. Quite frankly, my first impression was the same, but on reflection it is a fitting tribute to two men who went through their career with humility, a love of life and, above all, a dedication to their craft. I'm glad I had the opportunity to pay my respects to two gentle souls who taught me how to laugh.

SPIKE MILLIGAN

Creative spirit, surrogate brother

PROFILE

Born: (Terence Milligan) 16 April 1918

Place of Birth: Ahmednugar, India

While serving as a gunner in the Royal Artillery, Spike met Harry Secombe who after the war introduced him to scriptwriter Jimmy Grafton. Appreciating Spike's surreal talent, Grafton encouraged him in collaborations with two more of Secombe's friends – Michael Bentine and Peter Sellers – and the Goons were born.

Selected radio: *Opportunity Knocks* (1949), *Crazy People* (1951), *The Goon Show* (1952-60)

Selected films: *The Case of the Mukkinese Battlehorn* (1956), *Watch Your Stern* (1960), *The Magic Christian* (1970), *Adolf Hitler, My Part in His Downfall* (1972), *Digby, the Biggest Dog in the World* (1973), *The Three Musketeers* (1974), *The Great McGonagall* (1974), *The Last Remake of Beau Geste* (1977), *Yellowbeard* (1983)

Selected TV: *The Idiot Weekly, Price 2d* (1956), *A Show Called Fred* (1956), *Son of Fred* (1956), *The Telegoons* (1963-64), *The World of Beachcomber* (1968-69), *Curry and Chips* (1969), *Q...*(1969-82), *Oh in Colour*

(1970), *The Marty Feldman*   **Died:** 27 February 2002
Comedy Machine (1971-72),
An Evening with Spike Milligan
(1996)

Spike and I shared an office for over fifty years, so I ought to know him better than most people, but then again, how can one understand the workings of such a creative, tortured imagination that drove Spike in and out of darkness?

I'd heard of Spike long before our first meeting. He'd never written anything at that time or, to put it more accurately, he'd never written anything that was accepted by BBC Radio and transmitted. People spoke of him as eccentric, creative, and 'zany' – a word I've never understood or liked.

In 1951, propped up in my hospital bed awaiting a fairly serious operation and connected to the world through my headphones, I dozed through the news at six, which was the same as the news at one, followed by a talk on how to grow cabbages, followed by fifteen minutes of birdsong, followed by . . . I must have dozed then but was instantly alert when the opening music of a new comedy show exploded into my semi-consciousness. From the onset the show was fresh, funny, fast and took no prisoners. I must have laughed out loud at one stage because a nurse dashed into the room fearing the worst, but she was shushed out and sent packing. Exhausted with laughter I listened to the closing credits: script by Spike Milligan and Larry Stephens. I knew, without a shadow of a doubt, Spike and Larry were about to belong to our exclusive club of scriptwriters which at that time were as rare as a tie in a nudist camp.

So captivated was I by the joyful exuberance, the inventiveness, and the sheer disregard for any of the rules of broadcasting, I couldn't wait to write to let Spike and Larry know how uplifting it had been to listen to. I had only one criticism – nit-picking really, but in a way important – it was the title, *Crazy People*. Why should anything which did not conform be labelled crazy? If they were truly 'crazy people', give me a room in the asylum any day.

Three days later, my head swathed in bandages, groggy with the after-effects of the operation, I was propped up again by pillows, looking for all the world like an up-market charlady the morning after. The door was wedged open and nurses swept in and out, doing whatever nurses do, extraordinarily well. I gazed blearily towards the door and I saw two white faces peering in at me.

'I'm Spike Milligan and this is Larry Stephens.' They were waving a piece of paper. 'Got your letter,' he said, but at that moment the portly figure of the Matron arrived and they were ordered out. It was several catnaps, a bowl of soup and a visit from the surgeon before I suddenly realised that I'd just met Spike Milligan for the first time, and what a beginning to one of the most important happenings in my life.

Crazy People begat *The Goon Show* but, sadly, Larry Stephens, Spike's co-writer, died. Like most of us, he'd survived the war, having served in India, and his tragic early death reminded us all that time is not on anybody's side.

Spike took over the writing of *The Goon Show* and, with Peter Sellers and Harry Secombe, it took the listeners by the ears, lifting them into a new dimension. During the grim, blacked-out days of World War II, Ted Kavanagh entered the dark house of comedy with a box of matches and produced *ITMA*. It was only a glimmer of a light but it was better than nothing. In the first years of peace that followed, Frank Muir and Denis Norden discovered the dark house of comedy and, by candlelight, *Take It From Here* occupied the radio comedy output, followed by *Educating Archie*. More candles.

Other shows came along but 'The House of Comedy' needed electricity. Then, out of the blue. . . the Goons . . . Spike Milligan simply blew the roof off, and lit the whole place with sunshine.

At a cursory glance, *The Goon Show* was merely a quick-fire delivery of extremely funny lines mouthed by eccentric characters, but this was only the froth. *In The Goon Show*, Spike was unknowingly portraying every facet of the British psyche.

For instance, Neddy Seagoon, played by Harry Secombe, was the archetype of a section of hyper patriots, believing that everything that was British was superior to anything else in the world, politicians knew best and God had a room at Chequers. In fact, if the whole of this planet's population were British it would be paradise found.

Major Bloodnok was a dinosaur portraying a disreputable section of the establishment. These Bloodnoks only have to be summoned to a higher authority to deny strenuously that they had ever been in charge of the mess funds or 'I never met the lady!' In fact, he would, in a quick flash of panic, admit to several misdemeanours when in all probability 'higher authority' merely wished to invite him to tea. Incidentally, this 'higher authority' is not without its Bloodnoks.

Gritpipe Thynne, was a George Saunders soundalike, the brains behind numerous scurrilous adventures with the dirty work being carried out by his obtuse French 'Gofor' – Moriarty.

Eccles, well-meaning, good-natured and unthinking, another section of the British electorate – a gift to politicians as he signed his name with a cross. Bluebottle, every school bully's breakfast; the Cruns, elderly, innocent, incredible and in debt.

Add to that collection of individuals a brilliant riot of sound effects.

Originally, I posed the likely possibility that Spike created these characters unknowingly, but if he was aware of the enormous canvas he was painting he was more brilliant than I gave him credit for. Many would-be writers have endeavoured to emulate The Goons but there is only one Milligan. If you can't paint it's useless to try to copy Matisse.

Spike and I recognised in each other a kindred spirit and our careers would be run on parallel lines. With this in mind, we rented ourselves an office five floors above a greengrocer's shop. It wasn't in the best part of London – Shepherd's Bush, as a matter of fact – and it wasn't even furnished, but we soon sorted that out. Oh, happy days. In for a penny, in for a pound. We even had a telephone installed and spent many a dull moment in conversation with the speaking clock, even a wrong number would be a welcome diversion.

Gradually, however, real calls came in, then more calls, and within a few weeks we found ourselves a typist. When we interviewed her it should have been obvious that the only thing she was good at was interviews; she didn't seem to have worked much although she must have been pushing forty. Spike would dictate to her but she spent ages searching for the key she wished to start with, by which time Spike had forgotten what he was going to say, anyway.

We put her on to making the tea. That worked out fine

until one day Spike went to the toilet and found the basin full of tea leaves.

'Eric!' he shouted, and when I came in he pointed to the tea leaves. Over our shoulders peered our typist. She was petrified and reached out to flush them away but Spike stopped her and bent closer to gaze at the tea leaves. Then, after a few moments he turned to her and said in a grave voice, 'You are going on a long journey.' It was only a joke, but she went anyway, so Spike reclaimed his typewriter and once again the office rang out with the merry clack-clack of his two-fingered gavotte.

It was a fun time; we had to clamber over cases of fruit and veg before we began the five flights of uncarpeted stairs up to our office, and there were times when the grocer managed a new post-war fruit like bananas or pineapples. The jungle drums thumped out and before they'd finished there'd be a queue outside the shop, so when we arrived to go to our office we were hustled to the back of the queue! On one occasion the hopeful crowd for whatever was stretched so far down Shepherd's Bush that by the time we reached the shop and climbed the everlasting stairs it was time to come down again for lunch.

We enjoyed ourselves at Bertorellis, eating pasta washed down with a bottle of rough red wine, sometimes more than a bottle, and once, celebrating the end of one of our shows, we didn't leave till the early hours of the following day. Next to the restaurant was a Funeral Parlour and on one occasion Spike lay on the pavement, knocked on the door and shouted, 'Shop!' It was funny then, but it is as well to remember in those days it was a novelty to see people lying on the pavement.

The pressure, however, of writing *The Goon Show* single-handed was having its effect on Spike. The sheer momentum of the weekly turn-out became a burden too far and he asked me if I'd co-write it with him. I wasn't too busy at the time and it was clear to me that Spike was rushing downhill with no brakes. It was great for a few weeks, then came our first spat. It was silly, trivial, and should have died for lack of nourishment but it flared up. It was ludicrous, it was whether it should be 'the' or 'and', I can't remember what the actual word was, or whether it should be 'in' or 'out' or whatever it was. By now our voices had increased in volume as if we were conversing with each other across the River Thames. Suddenly Spike picked up a heavy paperweight and threw it at me. Had I dodged, ducked, taken evasive action, it would probably have killed me. As it was, I stood rooted to the spot with shock and it missed me by a mile, crashing through the window, hurtling down onto the pavement of Shepherd's Bush.

For a moment, we stared at each other in amazement. Then I went down to the street, brought back the guided missile which I plonked on Spike's desk, saying in a calm voice, 'Remember what date this was.' Pathetic and juvenile, Spike stared at me as if I'd just recited 'Humpty Dumpty', his eyes darting all over the place as if he was trying to remember where he was. His shirt was open at the neck and I noticed red spots on his chest which hadn't been there before. It was my first introduction to manic depression, an illness that was never more than an arm's length away throughout the rest of his life.

We are all subject to what we glibly call 'depression', but it is not really depression. We are down, saddened, or just plain bored, but any of these symptoms could scarcely be described as an illness; they are merely a condition. Manic depression, as far as I know, is incurable and if it came to having a leg off, or suffering as Spike did, give me a crutch every time.

I thoroughly enjoyed writing with him. It was a completely new and exciting experience for me. I was like a child on Christmas morning, taking his toys out of the box. Neddy, Bluebottle, the Cruns, all the characters so firmly established almost wrote themselves, our favourite being Bloodnok. So much so, we spent a whole morning laughing helplessly at the situation we'd written him into. Poor old Bloodnok, so transparent. Living by his wits was why he was always hungry – a born idiot.

F/X DOOR KNOCK
BLOODNOK Come in.
F/X DOOR OPENS
INSPECTOR Major Bloodnok?
BLOODNOK I'm not in, I mean how dare you break into my house I'm a respectable squatter.
INSPECTOR It's taken us months to track you down.
BLOODNOK It's all lies I tell you.
INSPECTOR Are you Dennis Bloodnok?
BLOODNOK No sir, I'm Arthur Bloodnok,
Dennis is my brother.
INSPECTOR Can you give me his address?
BLOODNOK No sir. I only see him once a year and he's just been.
INSPECTOR Pity, we'd like to trace him because an old relation has died leaving him a rather large legacy.

I must pause here because Spike and I knew what was coming and most of the script above is my own invention. We had stacks of other lines of dialogue. Each one had the tears rolling. We could have continued this interchange all day, but better was to come.

BLOODNOK A large legacy you say? How much?

INSPECTOR I'm afraid that is confidential between the distant relative and your brother, Dennis.

BLOODNOK Stap me spindles! Dennis just happens to be in the other room.

INSPECTOR You said you only met once a year.

BLOODNOK Yes, by a strange coincidence he came yesterday and he hasn't gone yet. I'll go and get him.

F/X DOOR OPENS THEN CLOSES

F/X DOOR REOPENS

BLOODNOK Ah, Inspector, my brother Arthur tells me you wish to see me on a monetary matter. I'm Dennis Bloodnok.

INSPECTOR You look extraordinarily like your brother.

BLOODNOK Yes, we're identical twins, born on the same day.

INSPECTOR How do I know you are Dennis Bloodnok?

BLOODNOK Of course I'm Dennis and if you don't believe me . . .

F/X DOOR OPENS DOOR CLOSES

BLOODNOK What's all this nonsense, Inspector? I'll not have you call my brother Dennis a liar.

F/X DOOR OPENS ETC.

Again, Spike and I could have written this scene ad infinitum but there were other characters in *The Goon Show* awaiting their turn, so sadly we had to pay off the sequence and we had to get back to work. After several hilarious suggestions, we settled for the Inspector insisting that in order to clear matters up it would be necessary to see the two brothers together at which Bloodnok was horrified. He begged the Inspector not to insist because they must never be seen together. The Inspector did insist, so sadly . . .

F/X DOOR OPENING DOOR CLOSING
F/X DOOR OPENING
BLOODNOK (walks in full of old madam announcing)
Here we are, now are you satisfied my dear fellow?
INSPECTOR (Baffled) But there's only one of you.
BLOODNOK Gad! The curse of the Bloodnok's has struck
again!

Those days in Shepherd's Bush were a joyous learning
curve and by the time we'd moved our offices to a more
salubrious part of Kensington High Street, scriptwriters
were springing up like weeds in a tip. We were happily
established a short walk from a Chinese restaurant which
we called our 'works canteen' but the roads were getting
busier, it became harder to park and when they decided
to build the Royal Garden Hotel opposite it was the last
straw. We upped sticks and moved to our present home
just off Bayswater Road. We had more space; it was quiet
and was an ideal place in which to grow old gracefully.
But in those days, growing old was for other people;
writing comedy is the great elixir of life and we lived out
our full share of it.

Spike then had his office just across the landing from
my office – only four paces away, but one morning there
was a knock at my door.

'Come in,' I said and Spike's secretary entered with
a sealed envelope addressed to me. She handed it over,
then I slit open the envelope, took out the letter and
read:

Dear Eric,
Do you fancy going to lunch?
Sincerely
Spike

So I got my secretary and dictated:

Dear Spike,

Yes, I fancy going to lunch. Where do you suggest?

Sincerely

Eric

She duly typed it and crossed the landing and delivered it to Spike. Two minutes later another missive:

Dear Eric,

I don't mind at all.

Sincerely

Spike

After a few more deliveries it was:

Dear Eric,

I think we should go soon.

Sincerely,

Spike

To which I dictated a rather curt:

Dear Spike,

Why?

This my secretary typed and delivered and almost before she had got back and settled down the door opened and Spike stood there.

He said, 'We've got to go now.'

I repeated, 'Why?' and Spike replied, 'I'm running out of paper.' It was a good lunch.

On another occasion he limped into the office, his face was scratched, his hands were leaking blood, and there was a great rent in his jacket.

'How's the other chap?' I said.

He didn't reply and I didn't push it. I knew he'd tell me. It isn't often you are attacked by a bear in Kensington but I couldn't think of any other logical explanation. Apparently he'd had a row with his wife who was driving him to work.

'And she hit you?' I said. He shook his head, not very hard in case it fell off.

'It wasn't that kind of row,' he said. 'I can just about stomach runner beans but not every day of the week.'

'And then she hit you?' I repeated.

'No,' he shouted. 'I got so fed up I opened the door and got out.'

Unfortunately, at the time they were bowling down the Bayswater Road at 40 miles an hour. I still shudder when I think of what might have happened had they been followed by a number 14 bus. He would have stood a better chance with the bear.

I've eulogised about *The Goon Show* because I believe that this brilliant radio show will be most remembered by Spike's millions of followers all over the world, but let us not forget his hilarious contribution to television. Seven series of *The Q Show*, a visual *Goon Show* in glorious Technicolor, forty-two half-hours which he not only wrote but led the cast of characters through each episode. That is what I would describe as a prodigious output.

During, after, and in between his television appearances, Spike's name topped the bill in a number of stage shows. *Oblomov* followed by *Son of Oblomov* at the Prince of Wales Theatre, a show in which he spent the best part in a huge bed. Little wonder he took sleeping pills at home.

During Spike's heavy schedule, I went to South Africa to do a show in Cape Town; good house, good food and, best of all, sunshine every day. I remember thinking at the time that a few months out here wouldn't do Spike any harm. Then, even as this thought came into view, Spike was striding towards me. Of all places and of all people, it was Stanley meeting Livingstone.

'It's about time you took a holiday,' were my first words.

'Holiday be buggered,' he said. 'I'm doing a one man show at The Seven Arts.'

And if you think that's enough for any man, he somehow found time to write over seventy books. What a monumental contribution from a man who, right to the end, was complaining if only he had a little more time.

Sleep well, Spike, you've earned it.

Finally I would like to mention Norma Farnes. She was his manager, his mentor, his guru, and friend for over thirty years. She looked after Spike. If they applauded, she smiled and joined in. On the other hand, if they were hostile, she'd stand in front of him and take the flak.

I know that, wherever Spike is, he will appreciate this last bit. I only hope it doesn't embarrass Norma.

PETER SELLERS

A Gulliver in Lilliput

PROFILE

Born: 8 September 1925

Place of Birth: Southsea, Hampshire, England

The son of vaudeville entertainers, Sellers' first stage appearance was at the age of two weeks. Attended dance classes and learned to play the drums. Drafted into the RAF during WWII where he eventually became a concert party entertainer.

Selected radio: *Show Time* (1948), *The Goon Show* (1952-1960)

Selected films: Over sixty movies made. *The Mouse That Roared* (1959), *I'm All Right Jack* (1959), *The Millionairess* (1960), *The Pink Panther* (1963), *Dr Strangelove* (1964), *What's New, Pussycat?* (1965), *The Magic Christian* (1969), *Murder by Death* (1976), *Being There* (1979), *The Fiendish Plot of Dr Fu Manchu* (1980)

Selected TV: *A Show Called Fred* (1956), *Son of Fred* (1956), *Six Five Special* (1958), *Dickie Valentine Show* (1958), *Telegoons* (1963), *Sykes* (1968), *Tale of Men's Shirts* (1968), *Michael Parkinson Meets the Goons* (1972), *Don Lane Show* (1980)

Died: 24 July, 1980

If I was writing a book entitled Comedy Impression-ists, Rory Bremner would feature in it. However, he wouldn't be number one. Peter Sellers would, in my book, take the gold and Rory I'm sure would agree.

Peter was uncanny; any character he chose to play he would be that person. During the early days of *Educating Archie*, Peter Brough was the ventriloquist and Archie was his dummy. As is suggested in the title, Archie was to be educated. His tutor was played by a top class comedy actor, Robert Morton. In the few weeks he was with the programme he established himself as a regular member of the team and then, sadly and quite suddenly, he died. He was a loveable, warm person and we all missed him terribly.

Some weeks later, I was in a restaurant having dinner with Peter Sellers – just the two of us. It was late in the evening and the place was dimly lit, no doubt being frequented by the people who wished to be discreet. Peter and I sat opposite each other at a table for two. I can't imagine what we were doing there; in those days I only had one foot on the ladder and Peter was still on the pavement. I'm not sure it wasn't our first meeting, certainly our first meal together. Suddenly I heard Robert Morton asking me how I was enjoying the meal. I dropped my knife and fork and looked round. Robert wasn't long gone but wherever he was he most definitely wasn't here. Robert spoke again and when I looked across the table I was aghast. The hair on the back of my neck stood out – Robert was actually sitting opposite me!

I stared at him, frozen, incapable of thought, trauma-tised. Mercifully Peter chuckled and with a great sigh of relief I realised it wasn't Robert at all, it was Peter. I knew in that moment Peter Sellers was destined for astronomical success. Not only was it Robert's voice but, by some alchemy beyond my limited intelligence, Peter had changed for that moment his metabolism – he was Robert Morton. In that moment, I knew that, although I'd already met many extremely talented top-of-the-bills, Peter Sellers would eventually surpass us all.

His first big break came in *The Goon Show*, it was an inspired piece of casting. His creation of most of the characters is now legendary and, although Spike Milligan wrote the scripts, his job of putting the flesh on Peter's character, in many cases, was a walk in the park. Spike and I shared an office in Shepherd's Bush and Peter popped in many times, and when he did very little work was done but a heck of a lot of laughs were had.

During this period another frequent caller, unknown to us and to this day a mystery, was a man about six foot two, bushy black beard, in his thirties, but the most eccentric thing about him: he always wore a Scout's uniform. Obviously not a Boy Scout, perhaps he was a Scout Master, or more likely he wasn't a Scout at all but had bought the uniform from some jumble sale or other. We never did find out but we enjoyed his visits, especially as he spoke in a very high-pitched, whiny voice and on one of these occasions Peter happened to walk in. After a few minutes listening to this overgrown apparition he had to go to the lavatory and when in there we could hear his stifled laughter. We explained to the Baden Powell look-alike that Peter was prone to fits and it would perhaps be better if he left so that we could lay Peter on his back and apply cold compresses. Disregarding his remark that he had a first-aid badge we ushered him down the stairs. When Peter came out, tears streaming down his face, he began to speak exactly like our Scout. He also gave him a name which is indelibly written in the book of 'Comedy Characters' – it was Bluebottle.

About this time I was responsible for the comedy in a pantomime at the London Palladium . . . *Mother Goose* starring Max Bygraves, Richard Hearne (Mr Pastry) and Peter Sellers playing the Squire. The show went extremely well but I knew Peter was getting restless doing the same things night after night and on one particular show that mischievous, devious gift possessing Peter took over and the Squire gave a hilarious performance as a crusty old Indian army blimp. It was nothing like the words I'd written for him but to me they were a great improvement. The audience thought so, too, and after I pulled myself together the black thoughts engulfed me. Knowing the strict discipline backstage at the Palladium the 'powers that be' would be on to Peter like a ton of bricks. I was right but Peter, undaunted, struggled up through the rubble, dusted himself off and gave exactly the same outrageous Indian army performance the following night. This time his dialogue was even funnier but this time there were no recriminations – nothing was said. Obviously the budding score of accountants emerging to run the industry must have decided it was cheaper to let Peter have his head than to purchase another ton of bricks. Peter had come out on top and that irascible Indian army wallah became Major Dennis Bloodnok – another wonderful, magical addition to *The Goon Show*.

There are 'bread and butter' actors; then there are actors with talent which they use to great effect; then we come to a higher strata, the Peter Sellers class, blessed with exceptional talent. The difference is in the gift that used Peter Sellers – and extracted such a very high price for its services.

For example, when Peter Sellers played a part in a film he didn't leave the character in his dressing room at the end of the day's filming, he took it home with him.

If he was playing a shifty-eyed gangster, he was still a shifty-eyed gangster as long as the film lasted, and God help anybody who crossed him. I was lucky enough to be in *Heavens Above* with him, in which he played a clergyman, a person too kind-hearted, in fact much too good, to be a vicar. After a day's filming he would go home cheerful, God fearing and goodwill to all men. Many a beggar must have thought it was Christmas as Peter stuffed a fiver into his hand and he probably gave him a Blessing for good measure. He was a wonderful companion to all and sundry for a couple of months.

Then he starred as Doctor Strangelove, a sinister, menacing character and for the duration of that film people made themselves scarce. This was the price of his demanding gift. Were it possible for Peter to make nothing but happy, smiling films like *Heavens Above* all his life, he would certainly have been canonised.

One of Peter's hobbies was motor cars or, to be more precise, it wasn't just a hobby, it was a mania . . . in fact, he kept the car industry solvent for years. It wasn't difficult for Peter to trade in his current transport because they rarely had more than twenty miles on the clock. On one particular day Peter was driving his latest acquisition, a Mercedes Benz (having got bored with his Rolls which he'd had for nearly a week). Next to him sat Graham Stark, an actor friend of Peter's. Not just a friend, a devoted fan, indeed had Peter asked him to jump off Waterloo Bridge there'd be no hesitation. In half an hour Graham would have been floating into the English Channel. However, on this bright summer's day he was in seventh heaven bowling along in a new Mercedes Benz with Peter at the wheel.

His happy thoughts were interrupted when Peter said, 'Can you hear a squeak, Graham?'

Graham listened attentively and, after a time, he replied, 'No, Peter, I can't.' But Peter wasn't satisfied. He pulled into a lay-by and asked Graham if he wouldn't mind sitting in the back seat in case the offending squeak was at the rear. After another mile, he stopped again and Graham leaned forward saying there was no squeak at the back. Peter insisted there was a squeak and would Graham mind getting into the boot of the car where the squeak might be more audible? Graham hopped in the boot willingly and Peter drove off again, the miles went by, then just ahead he spotted an old English pub and, deciding he could do with a bevy, he pulled into the fore-court.

The landlord was overwhelmed, firstly by the brand new Merc and now Peter Sellers, whom he recognised, was enjoying a pint of old English ale in his pub. Feeling peckish, Peter also enjoyed a ploughman's lunch. Meanwhile, the landlord, who had been making a slow admiring circle round the Mercedes Benz, burst back into his pub and told Peter there was a frantic knocking coming from the boot of his car. Peter, opening it, stared into Graham's white face then turned to the landlord and said, 'I'm taking my son to school' and, slamming the boot shut, drove off.

His addiction to cars wasn't restricted to the high quality of Rolls Royce and Mercedes Benz, it might be a passing Dormobile or a Reliant Robin, in fact anything on wheels that didn't involve pedalling. Peter and I did many one-hour comedy shows together and on each occasion he turned up in some different make of trans-port. Nothing surprised me until, for one show, he turned up in a Bubble car, a novel, tiny thing that had taken Peter's fancy that morning. So enthusiastic was he that we didn't start the final day's rehearsal until he'd taken me on a demonstration spin. I wasn't a nervous passenger but when we pulled up at traffic lights and a double-decker bus pulled alongside my heart rate doubled – my head didn't come up to the bus driver's feet!

Nervously, I said, 'What happens if he can't see us and he turns right?'

Peter was unperturbed. 'You're insured, aren't you?' he said.

When we finally arrived back at the Wood Green Empire he refused to leave it in the street, but had them open the scene dock so he could drive onto the backstage. At the time we were doing a live show and it had already started and as I was reaching the door handle Peter shot forward and drove onto the stage. It was a novel entrance and we were applauded when we stepped out. My first thought was, 'What do we do now?' After all, it was my show and Peter was the guest star.

When he was with me I never wrote our opening spot, we went through it on a wing and a prayer, surprising the producer, the floor manager and in some cases me. For instance, Peter would suggest something like he'd be sitting at an easel painting the audience. I was to tell jokes and Peter would explain to them he had been commissioned to paint them but it was important they were laughing as he painted. A simple idea, but in Peter's hands, hilarious. But entering in a Bubble car was something I never envisaged. It was a good entrance but what now? After the applause died down, Peter extolled the virtues of the Bubble car, then he began an auction with the audience. When he accepted the final bid, which was three times the car's worth, he announced the winner, who came on stage expecting Peter to hand him the keys. But that wasn't the pay-off. Peter shook him by the hand and congratulated him on winning, but the prize was not the car, it was two free tickets to next week's show.

There are some people who have sought to denigrate Peter, dwelling only on his darker side but, believe me, the driving force in him gave us more pleasure and entertainment than ever came from his detractors.

He will always be, to me, a Gulliver in Lilliput.

JOHNNY SPEIGHT

A golden nugget in a sieve full of writers

PROFILE

Born: 2 June 1920

Place of Birth: Canning Town, East London

A docker's son, Johnny originally dreamed of being a jazz drummer and played with the Syncopated Rhythm Boys before forming Johnny Speight and His Hot Shots. Assorted day jobs took a back seat when, in 1955, he was introduced to Frankie Howerd and taken on as a sketch writer for Howerd's radio show.

Selected radio: *The Frankie Howerd Show*

Selected theatre: *The Thoughts of Chairman Alf*

Selected films: *Till Death Us Do Part* (1968), *The Alf Garnett Saga* (1972)

Selected TV: *Two's Company* (1956), *The Arthur Haynes Show* (1957-66), *Sykes* (1960), *Till Death Us Do Part* (1965-75), *Curry and Chips* (1969), *Spooner's Patch* (with Ray Galton) (1979-82), *Till Death…*(1981), *The Lady is a Tramp* (1983-84), *In Sickness and in Health* (1985-92), *The Nineteenth Hole* (1989)

Died: 6 July 1998

It is not necessary to appear on stage, or stand in front of a television camera, to become one of my Comedy Heroes. What about the writers of comedy who provide the situations and the words that help to make good comedians great ones?

Johnny Speight will always be remembered as the writer who shot Arthur Haynes to fame in a situation comedy, elevated Warren Mitchell and Dandy Nichols to the top of the ratings in *Till Death Us Do Part* and *In Sickness and In Health*.

My dear friend Johnny Speight who, in my opinion, was the most brilliant and prolific master of his craft also wrote a series for Spike Milligan and myself entitled *Curry and Chips*, and a series on the troubled life of a golf secretary. In *The Nineteenth Hole* I played the hard-pressed, incompetent golf secretary and enjoyed it so much Johnny rewrote it for the stage. Bill Kenwright, who was putting on the show, didn't even want to see a script such was Johnny's reputation. All Bill said was, 'When do you want to do it?' So we did it and a good time was had by all.

Although Johnny was mainly known for his comedy scripts, there was another aspect of his talent – he was also a playwright. His dramas, which were sombre, dark and menacing, dealt with the mental instability of his unfortunate characters. His plays include: *The Salesman* starring Ian Holm and *The Knacker's Yard*. Leonard Rossiter and Bob Hoskins starred in his play *If There Weren't Any Blacks You'd Have To Invent Them*, and if that wasn't enough, Michael Caine and Frank Finlay starred in *The Compartment* and *The Playmates*.

All this prodigious output from a man selling insurance when we first met. How did this extraordinary person begin his career? In the early days B.T.G.S., 'Before *The*

Goon Show', Frankie Howerd, Spike and myself decided to form a company which would be called 'Associated London Scripts'. Two apprentice writers had just moved in with us above the greengrocer's shop office in Shepherd's Bush, so we invited them to join us. They were Alan Simpson and Ray Galton; at least we had a quorum if nothing else.

At the time, the BBC at last accepted the obvious, the staring-them-in-the-face fact that if they were to maintain their top of the league status in television, scriptwriters would have to be number-one priority. Incidentally, the BBC had no opposition in those days, no ATV, no ITV and certainly no Satellite. Rupert Murdoch had just left school.

I was asked to attend a meeting with the panjandrums of the BBC at Lime Grove, White City; the present outlet for BBCTV was still on the drawing board. The meeting was concerning the amount of comedy material needed to appease the voracious appetite of weekly television and, before I'd taken my first sip of lukewarm whatever it was, the spokesman blurted out, 'We need to find new writers' and they all stared at me as if I knew where to look. I replied to the effect that once television was established they would be inundated with scripts, jokes, ideas. What I didn't add was that when the avalanche came would they have anyone competent enough to separate the wheat from the chaff? Incidentally this thought had given birth to 'Associated London Scripts' and when our new company became known we weren't inundated by an avalanche of scripts, more a gentle snowfall, but in the first sprinkling was a crock of gold by a certain Johnny Speight.

His script was absolutely scintillating, a situation that moved on at pace and lines of dialogue screaming out to be performed. Luckily there was a telephone number on the front page and hours later Johnny, dressed in what must have been his best suit, and Connie, his wife, were standing in our office looking a little frightened. After all, you don't expect Spike Milligan and Eric Sykes to go crawling over sacks of vegetables and fruit before attacking five flights of stairs to a barely furnished office. It didn't seem to bother Johnny as much; he'd have come here had we been operating from a tent on Shepherd's Bush Green. Having confidence in his work, he was in a state of euphoria that we had confidence as well.

As it was opening time, I put on my overcoat and took them both to the pub and in half-an-hour John had made up his mind to pack in his job as a seller of insurance. The next morning he was crawling over the sacks of vegetables and fruit, making his way upstairs to the land of dreams. It was all very well for me to ask Johnny to pack in his insurance business, but now he needed money and, thankfully, the BBC wanted to do a series with Frankie Howerd. As I was up to my eyes with *Educating Archie* I couldn't script the Frank series at the same time, so the BBC were reluctant to proceed. But it gave me an idea. I suggested Johnny Speight, Simpson and Galton, three hopefuls yet to be bloodied. This the BBC agreed but only on the proviso that I would edit the show. I gave a sigh of relief, remembering Connie's white, worried face. Johnny would at least now have a wage packet. I felt like a camel having two tons of fruit lifted off its back. The experience of writing a weekly series would be invaluable and at least Connie Speight would have butter on the table and with my faith in John – jam as well!

Before long, John was not only established, but respected, moving inexorably to the top of the writing fraternity and the amazing output of the man is all the more remarkable when compared with today's contributions where scriptwriters outnumber the cast and additional dialogue is by . . . almost as many as the audience. If John had been born in the nineteenth century Charles Dickens would have had some opposition and Johnny could well be recommended reading in schools today.

He will mostly be remembered for his 'Alf Garnet' character: a bigot, a political misfit, a chauvinistic, domineering loudmouth. But his misguided rantings and his convoluted philosophising always hit the mark and that is what kept the 'Garnet' character fresh and up to date. For example, one week Garnet would be lambasting the Health Service and its shortcomings, again it was so beautifully scripted by Johnny it still appeared to be a show full of laughs but, by jingo, the shafts had found their mark. Arrowheads coated in the bombastic utterances, raising laughs, belying the intended targets. In fact, a close friend of ours, John Ballantyne a prominent ENT surgeon now retired, rang me after watching the show and eulogised, amazed at how accurate were Johnny's facts in portraying the over-burdened nurses and doctors at the sharp end, out-numbered by the armies of bureaucrats that were replacing the Matrons trained for many years to run hospitals for the benefit of the patients and not statistics.

There is also a stage musical John wrote: *Goebbels' Diaries*. It was an everyday story of life in the Reich Chancellery during World War II. It was written for Spike Milligan and myself, Spike playing Hitler and me the club-footed Goebbels, Minister of Propaganda for the Third Reich. It was brilliantly funny, Goebbels the Machiavellian manipulator behind Hitler suggesting ludicrous proposals to him i.e. why shouldn't the Führer make

World War II into a limited company, thereby entering all the expenses, artillery, ammunition, aircraft, in fact all the expenditure would be under the legal directorship of Adolf Hitler? His salary and his expense account would be astronomical and, as an added bonus, arrangements must be made to marry his girlfriend, Eva Braun, in order to put the whole enterprise in his wife's name . . . and so it goes on. Sadly, it was never performed. I doubt whether more than half a dozen people have ever seen it but, believe me, it would have lifted John onto a new pedestal.

He wrote mainly from home, using all the technology afforded by computer, enabling him to put millions of words onto compact discs and, in all probability, his life's work could be carried around in a medium sized suitcase. However, in spite of all the technology at his fingertips, his most valuable asset without a doubt was his wife, Connie.

I shudder when I think back to that first day when Johnny decided to give up his job and leap into the unknown; what was going through Connie's panic-stricken mind?

Whatever it was, she had faith in Johnny and took the leap with him – thank you, Connie.

JACQUES TATI

The ultimate master of laughs without words

PROFILE

Born: (Jacques Tatischeff) 9 October 1909

Place of Birth: Le Pecq Yvelines, France

A descendant of the Russian aristocracy, Jacques was born to Dutch and Russian parents and enjoyed a privileged upbring-ing. His first job was helping his father in the family picture framing business but it was sport that unwittingly shaped his future career.

Young Jacques used to mime his sporting activities to his team-mates who suggested he put his talents on the Paris stage. After years in music-halls, he began to write and direct his own comedy films.

Selected films: *Jour de Fête* (1949), *Monsieur Hulot's Holiday* (1952), *Mon Oncle* (1958), *Play-time* (1968), *Traffic* (1971)

Died: 4 November 1982

In my opinion the English and the French film industries turn out the best silent comedies in the world. I may be sticking my neck out because I've never watched Chinese films, or Russian, and nothing at all out of Africa. It may be because there's so little to amuse one in any of these places.

For my money, France takes top spot thanks to the inimitable Jacques Tati, a silent filmmaker of classic comedies that must undoubtedly be shown time and time again, and then some, all over the world. This is probably why thousands of asylum seekers are so desperate to live in the chaotic, funny world of Jacques' creations.

In his films we see his progression from sheer fun to a more serious side of life. The first of his films that I ever saw was entitled *Jour de Fête*. A hapless postman on a bicycle is played by Jacques himself, and what a hilarious performance. Many who remember *Jour de Fête* think back on it with a smiling fondness. In the camera it was ground shattering, a comedy film of truly international proportions.

His next offering was more constructive – *Monsieur Hulot's Holiday*: the accident-prone Monsieur Hulot was played by Jacques himself. This film, incidentally, I have seen six times and on each occasion I discovered some new piece of visual humour I'd missed.

Perhaps I can explain two of the opening scenes. Firstly, the journey to the holiday resort, a high shot of a railway station, the platform, a large group of holiday-makers crowded onto one platform, an unintelligible announcement at the end of which the whole crowd en masse disappears to the underground and we see them reappear on another platform. Again, unintelligible tannoy announcement and the crowd repeats the last exercise only to emerge onto a different platform. Finally, the train arrives and stops at the platform where they started from . . . pandemonium. All this was shot using one high-angled camera.

In a further episode we see the holidaymakers using the roads as a means of transport to the seaside. Again a high shot of a bend on the cobbled road of a small village sleeping under a hot sun, the only sign of life a huge shaggy dog dozing in the middle of the road. We hear a pre-emptive blare of a car horn approaching and the old creature creaks slowly to its feet and moves painfully to the pavement. Then a limousine sweeps round the corner and continues, the old dog limps back to the centre of the cobbles and resettles itself. The action from another car horn is repeated, car goes through, dog regains his place in the middle of the road and flops down. We hear another car horn but this time it's a feeble toy-town hooter reminiscent of Noddy's yellow car. This time, however, the dog stays put and the ancient rattle-trap of Monsieur Hulot's car is forced to stop in order not to run over the dog. After several ineffectual peeps on his horn he is forced to get out of his car, lift the old dog up, depositing it on the pavement in order to continue his journey.

In the holiday resort itself Jacques exploited various exquisitely drawn characters, such as an American businessman whose umbilical chord was the telephone to America. Then there was the old English couple, always first into meals, the wife imperiously strutting through her holiday while her husband followed meekly in her wake. The hotel was on the beach and during the whole film we were treated to a cast of hilarious characters, all together and yet completely divided.

In Jacques' next film, *Mon Oncle*, the message was all about the 'haves and the have-nots'. It was still a comedy masterpiece, although the social comment was increasing, and in his next film again the message was poking its head above the comedy.

I didn't know Jacques very well but when we first met he made my year when he told me he had enjoyed my silent movie *The Plank* at the Cannes Film Festival. It is moments like this when someone you have idolised makes you feel your life hasn't been entirely in vain.

After this meeting we met only twice – at the premier of his last two pictures in which he arranged that we sat together. On the first occasion, before the lights went down, he whispered to me, 'Everybody is saying "who's that tall, lanky fellow sitting next to Eric Sykes?" ' That was the kind of man he was.

As the lights went up when the film ended I poured out the usual clichés, 'brilliant', 'superb', etc. He looked at me for a moment, then he said, 'But you didn't laugh.'

'Was I meant to?' I replied.

It was a precocious remark on my part and the moment it emerged I was appalled at my own temerity. I remember those exact words and I will never forget my immediate feeling of regret at having responded in this glib, cavalier fashion. After all, he was Jacques Tati and I had just watched his film. It was like a guest at the dinner table complaining that the Chablis was warm.

Jacques stared at me for a moment, ignoring other fans wanting to congratulate him on yet another triumph. Why hadn't I just joined the rest of them in sugary expressions of praise? But then my fears were swept away.

When, in between signing one of the bits of paper, he murmured, 'I appreciate what you said. It wasn't one of my best efforts.'

It was only later, having had a deeper discussion, I was immensely relieved that he hadn't taken offence at my remarks. After all, you don't tell Michael Schumacher how to drive!

I was, and am, totally dedicated to a comedy that induces people to laugh, not chuckle or titter or, at worst, snigger, but to throw back their heads in a joyous burst of capitulation. During our discussion I mentioned to Jacques that his first film, *Jour de Fête*, was complete bliss, the hapless postman cycling his erratic course through a French village, followed by *Monsieur Hulot's Holiday*. Then, from *Mon Oncle* to all his subsequent films the social messages were gaining strength.

Jacques is one of the very few people fully to understand what makes people laugh, to be able to portray visual comedy that transcends boundaries of race, colour or creed and I was afraid that this Master was diluting his comedy with social comment. We are inundated with people spouting about social injustice at the drop of a hat in Parliament, television, radio, soap boxes, pubs and almost any place where there is someone to listen. But the listeners don't laugh and genuine laughter is the most precious gift we possess.

In England we were unfortunate inasmuch we didn't have the opportunity to watch Jacques live on stage. Some time ago I saw an old clip from a French television channel showing Jacques performing a hilarious three minutes from his stage act. He tiptoed onto the circus arena, black frock coat, riding boots, top hat. With crop in hand, turning to the audience he doffed his top hat, bowed and with a flick of his riding crop executed a complicated routine in the dressage section of a gymkhana. He backed up, then cantered forward in a steady trot, reared, turned in circles, all under the gentle control of his riding crop. It was a masterly exhibition of horsemanship. Indeed, there was only one thing missing:

a horse. Sheer magic, sophisticated and dignified, it was as refreshing as a pint of water in the Gobi desert.

Up until I watched this short television extract I'd thought of Jacques Tati purely as a filmmaker but then why should I have been so surprised? His mastery of visual comedy could only have begun in the music hall. Stan Laurel's humour was nurtured and polished in the music hall before he ever stepped in front of a camera.

Strangely enough, one of my original 'Comedy Heroes' was an act simply billed as 'Sherkot'. I saw him on stage in 1938 and the utter simplicity of his presentation grabbed me before he made his appearance. An empty stage, goal posts in the centre in front of a backcloth of a massed football crowd, Sherkot bounded on and took his place in the goalmouth, flat cap, polo-necked sweater, gloves, shorts (long ones) in fact any goalkeeper of the period. Jumping up and down, touching the crossbar loosening up before we heard a whistle for the kick off. From then on he was diving for saves, picking up imaginary balls from inside the goal and cheeking the crowd on the backcloth.

You can imagine that, without a spoken word, it was the hit of the evening. Why then does he not warrant space to himself in this book? After proposing him as one of my Comedy Heroes, the publishers said, 'Who's Sherkot?' My office had never heard of anyone called Sherkot, taxi drivers notorious for knowing everything were mystified when I mentioned Sherkot, till in the end I began to believe he must have been a figment of my imagination. So I dropped him.

Later, when I was just finishing my eulogies to Jacques Tati, I had a sudden inspiration. If any man alive had heard of Sherkot besides me it would have to be my old mate Denis Norden. I rang him and in the course of our conversation I casually remarked, 'Did you ever hear of a music hall act called Sherkot?'

Quick as a pickpocket he replied, 'Yes, Sherkot the goal keeper with a backcloth of spectators.' He was so enthusiastic describing Sherkot's antics in goal that I began to be sorry I'd left this funnyman out of the book, but after Denis finished waxing lyrical over Sherkot he said, 'Of course you know that it wasn't his act? he'd knocked it off, backcloth, goals, the lot, from Jacques Tati.'

Well done, Sherkot. It was a good try.

Thank you, Jacques, for another glimpse at another sparkling facet of your dominance in bringing happiness wherever your gems are shown.

TERRY THOMAS

Always the same character and always funny

PROFILE

Born: (Thomas Terry Hoar-Stevens) 14 July 1911

Place of Birth: Finchley, London

After working as a clerk, meat salesman, pianist, bandleader, music-hall comedian and movie extra, Terry's career took off after the Second World War when he established himself in films and became one of Britain's first TV comedy stars.

Selected radio: *Variety Bandbox* (1946-50), *Town with Terry* (1948-49), *Top of the Town* (1953-55)

Selected theatre: *Piccadilly Hayride* (1947-48), *Room for Two* (1955), *Large as Life* (1957)

Selected films: *Private's Progress* (1956), *Blue Murder at St Trinian's* (1957), *The Naked Truth* (1958), *Carlton Browne of the FO* (1958), *I'm All Right, Jack* (1959), *School for Scoundrels* (1960), *It's a Mad, Mad, Mad World* (1963), *How to Murder Your Wife* (1965), *Those Magnificent Men in Their Flying Machines* (1965), *Monte Carlo or Bust!* (1969), *The Abominable Dr Phibes* (1971), *The Bawdy Adventures of Tom Jones* (1976)

Selected TV: *How Do You View?*
(1949-53), *Around the Town*
(1955), *Strictly T-T* (1956), *Beat
Up the Town* (1957), *The Old
Campaigner* (1968), *The Dickie
Henderson Show* (1971)

Died: 8 January 1990

In about 1955 I wrote a television half-hour for Terry Thomas. It was a pilot show that unfortunately crash landed, in other words it never saw the light of day, only the inside of a dustbin. I was upset because I knew it had nothing to do with Terry; the script was pathetic, much as I patched and altered and tried to breathe life into a terminal case during rehearsals. I could only apologise afterwards to Terry for lumbering him with a no-hoper.

A lesser person might have ranted, lashed out or, even worse, ignored me at the bar. Terry did none of these things. To him it was all part of life's rich pageant. He listened to my apologies, then put his arm round my shoulders and, with his gap-toothed smile, he said, 'Never mind, there'll be other times.'

His words were prophetic. In 1958 we both appeared in a revue starring Harry Secombe, a marvellous funny man. This Palladium show may have looked bright, breezy and carefree from an audience point of view, but backstage discipline was strict. A small misdemeanour would have been blown into an international crisis and, although outwardly relaxed, most of us tiptoed through this minefield of authority until whatever disaster was averted and we were back to the happy- go-lucky attitude that whatever occurred, it was nothing a large brandy couldn't cure. From the stage manager in the front line in the prompt corner, to the top-drawer managers of the house wearing dinner jackets and plastic smiles, between them they ran the Palladium like a house of correction. Without exception we all trod warily. All, that is, except Terry Thomas. He was much admired by most of the cast for his sheer contempt for the strict rules administered by people for whom he had little regard.

I recollect on one occasion when Terry was late for his entrance. He wasn't flustered, not in the least. In the same predicament we would have rushed to the stage as if the dressing room was on fire, but we didn't happen to be Terry. As he strolled nonchalantly to the wings the stage manager in a red boiled rage was about to blow him to smithereens, Terry calmly lit his cigarette and inserted it into his amber cigarette holder. It was too much for the poor stage manager who could only splutter incoherently. Terry raised his hand and said quietly, 'You're not doing your blood pressure any good, old boy.' And with that he calmly walked on the stage to do his act.

Those Magnificent Men in Their Flying Machines is a classic film still shown to this day on television. It was a magical experience working with Terry who played an aristocratic black sheep with a passion for flying old rattle traps through the air. I was cast as his hapless, downtrodden valet/chauffeur and the active, dangerous perpetrator of his many dastardly, nefarious schemes. It wasn't just a film, it was an epic and with Terry, a glorious slice of life, bearing out my theory that films should be made and not seen.

By this time Terry was an international film actor usually playing the same role in each production, a character many have tried to emulate, alas falling well short of the original.

One shot in the film *Those Magnificent Men in Their*

Flying Machines was a long shot of a French racecourse with Terry and me in the foreground. Naturally with nearly a thousand extras – strolling crowds of elegantly dressed Edwardian fops escorting their ladies with parasols. To dress extras was a phenomenal feat, then to instruct them by megaphone what they were expected to do and to light the scene must have given the cameraman insomnia. Terry and I were not yet in position, but I noticed the director was getting a little agitated at the time it was taking to get everything in order for us to take our positions. Eventually, however, and three hours late, we stood on our marks in the foreground while the massive crowd behind us waited for the 'Action'. All was quiet, everything was set to roll when Terry, shielding his eyes against the lights, looked up at Ken Annakin, the director, sitting fifteen feet in the air on the camera crane.

'Yes, Terry,' said Ken.

Terry took the cigarette holder from his mouth and said, 'Ken, old boy, before we shoot I'd just like to have a few words with Eric.'

Ken nodded, the first assistant picked up his megaphone and shouted, 'Relax, everybody' and a thousand extras sagged with relieved tension. In the meantime, Terry led me to the car park some two hundred yards away out of sight of the film set. Then Terry opened the boot of his car, turned to me and said, 'What would you like to drink?' I couldn't believe it, his car boot was better stocked than some of the clubs in St James's Square.

'I'll have a gin and tonic,' I said. Terry poured out a generous measure in a cut glass tumbler and, nonchalantly, he asked, 'Lemon?' and when I nodded he sliced a lemon and in two minutes we were sitting comfortably in the little space by the bar in his boot. I suddenly remembered the large crowd relaxing, the director looking at his watch, and the lighting cameraman staring through a piece of smoked glass at the sun.

'Terry,' I said, 'what did you want to talk to me about?'

Coolly, he replied, 'Nothing, old boy, I thought we could both do with a drink.'

Is it any wonder I enjoyed working with him?

He made films for different film companies all over the world but it was the same part, whether it be an Earl or a Duke, Ambassador or Diplomat. The social status of each role was always the same. In each role he was either shifty, fawning, or inept. It was a character he played with grace and panache. In real life, however, he was none of these. He enjoyed portraying the characters but, after all, they were his livelihood and, believe me, he needed money in order to keep up his lifestyle off stage.

For instance, we were in a film together being shot at Di Laurentis Studios in Rome on a schedule of eleven weeks. Naturally, watching the pennies, I stayed at a modest hotel: clean, good food and most of all affordable. Not in Terry's class. He had a suite in one of the better hotels just off the Via Veneto, accepting the bows of the staff as his birthright and, while I took a taxi and my life in my hands to the studio, Terry was driven through the gates in a white Rolls Royce which he'd hired for the full eleven weeks. No wonder the commissionaire at the gate saluted him every morning. Most weekends we flew back to England on Alitalia. Terry never ate the usual plastic food served up, instead his custom was to board the aircraft with a small wicker hamper which he handed over to the stewardess. The basket usually contained cold chicken, salad and a bottle of Pouilly Fuise which was served up to him at meal time. I've no doubt that if he had asked for the chicken to be roasted, they would have deemed it an honour to cook it.

After a few of these flights, Terry phoned me at home on the Sunday.

'Eric, dear boy,' he said. I smiled; it was always amusing just to hear him speak, as if every word had been strained through a silk cloth before it emerged. 'Eric, dear boy,' he said. 'I've taken the liberty of changing our flight tomorrow. We're now booked out on South African Airways – it will be more comfortable and the first stop is Rome, et voila'.

I thanked him and as we boarded the South African Airways flight he was treated with deference, me less so as they probably had the impression I was his valet. As that was the part I was playing in the film, in a way it was a good rehearsal. As we strapped ourselves in I noticed he hadn't brought his little basket of cold chicken.

'No need,' he replied as I asked him about it. 'This airplane is a long haul flight to South Africa – better food, better accommodation and a smooth journey.'

As always he hit the nail bang on its head.

I have a feeling that, had he been invited to Buckingham Palace, the Queen would have stood when he entered the room.

WILSON, KEPPEL & BETTY

Sand in my shoes from the Sahara, no less

PROFILE

Jack Wilson
Born: 29 January 1894

Place of Birth: Liverpool

Joe Keppel
Born: 10 May 1895

Place of Birth: Cork, Ireland

Jack and Joe met in the US in 1919 when they formed a tap dancing duo and in 1928 teamed up with American Betty Knox who had been Jack Benny's vaudeville partner. The trio created their famous 'Cleopatra's Nightmare' routine and came to England in 1932. When Betty retired in 1941 to become a journalist, her seventeen-year-old daughter Patsy took her place. Further Bettys followed before the act was disbanded in 1963.

Selected theatre: *Royal Variety Performances* (1934, 1945, 1947)

Selected films: *On the Air* (1934)

Jack Wilson died: 24 August 1970
Joe Keppel died: 15 August 1977
Betty Knox died: late 1950s

Many years ago, I met Wilson, Keppel and Betty at the Bristol Hippodrome. They were old men by this time. In fact, when I saw them at Bristol, the Betty of the act was the granddaughter of the original Betty.

In the old days, it was the custom for acts to go to the theatre every morning, some to collect any mail and for the speciality act it was a gruelling rehearsal period. Everyone seemed to find space, perhaps in a corner of the stage a juggler throwing half a dozen clubs in a parabolic of perfection . . . parents walking slowly on either side of a two-year-old in a harness tumbling and back-flipping in no danger of mishap as Mum and Dad held each end of the harness – hopefully, in later years, the tot would be a valuable asset to the family of acrobats . . . a unicyclist weaving in and around the organised mayhem.

At one o'clock the rehearsals were over and the theatre closed until the evening show. Some of the acts went back to their digs for lunch, others went to the billiard halls and invariably the comics went to the pub. It was there I first had a chat with Wilson and Keppel, who had only popped in and out of the stage door to collect any letters, no need to rehearse. I should imagine the last time they went through their routine was probably to acquaint Betty number two with her part in the act.

Sadly, going back over fifty years, I've forgotten their Christian names. To me they will always be Wilson, Keppel and Betty. The pub was practically empty when I walked in, but my heart leapt when I turned round to spot them sitting at a table, half pints before them, Wilson in a trilby, and Keppel in a flat cap. They were sitting straight-backed, arms folded looking straight ahead at nothing.

Now, as I am writing about them, I seem to recall that

one of them was Jack. He was the talkative one and when I offered to buy them a drink Jack said, 'I'll have the other half,' then he nodded towards Keppel, saying, 'Don't get him one, he's had enough,' It was like sitting in Madame Tussauds opposite two of the exhibits. We sat in silence for at least two more half-pints before Jack said, 'Cheers,' and I replied, 'Cheers,' glad of a chat. It might sound like a dull h'appeth but for me I was spellbound. It's not every day one is within touching distance of your heroes.

They were not mobbed, besieged by fans, swamped by a daily post-box from admirers all over the world, because they only came to life on stage, and off it they were invisible and forgettable. Perhaps in the days of Queen Victoria they were young tearaways off stage but the act would be exactly the same routine, the only difference being their age.

But it speaks for itself that Wilson, Keppel and Betty began their career about a hundred years ago and, to my knowledge, not one bar of music, nor one of their pace steps, nor their style of presentation had been altered. This is a great compliment to my heroes. Why paint a horse behind Mona Lisa, isn't she enough? Their act was simple, costumed exactly as the frescoes in the tombs of the ancient Egyptians. The one-sided character reminded one of Picasso's later sketches.

After sprinkling sand on the floor, Wilson and Keppel did a hilarious parody of the ancient Egyptians doing a sand dance, back and forward they went to each four bars, perfectly synchronised. It was the funniest part of their act and is the bit most filmed for the archives, but obviously the few minutes of this immortal eccentric dance was hardly an act and this is where Betty came in to begin her dance of the seven veils whilst Wilson and Keppel sat cross-legged in the foreground, accompanying Betty on their flutes, getting more excited as the veils were removed and, naturally, there was a blackout before the seventh veil revealed all!

During that Bristol week I watched them every night, not the whole act but I wouldn't miss the opening sand dance for a standing ovation. When the front cloth came down at the end of the act they hurried back on stage to sweep up the sand and pour it back into what looked remarkably like a pewter coffee pot. When this was done, they folded their tap board into a three-foot square and they were ready for the second house during which the opposite occurred. When the front cloth was down they rushed onto the stage, unfolded their tap board and when whoever was performing in front finished his act the curtain would go up and on came Wilson and Keppel, the act everyone was waiting for. Back and forward they danced, Jack in front sprinkling the sand from the coffee pot, and into their routine. At the end of their act when the curtain came down, they rushed on stage sweeping the sand into the pot, then they folded up their tap board and carried it off. As Jack passed me in the wings he hissed, 'We've had that same sand for thirty-eight years.'

I said, 'Don't you ever change it?'

He said, 'We did – thirty-eight years ago. This lot's special – it's from the Sahara'.

Whether he was telling the truth or being humorous I'll never know; had he said that Queen Victoria was his Auntie I would have believed it.

One gets the feeling their music score, unchanged for over sixty years, was written on parchment, same dance steps, same tap boards, same sand . . . possibly from the Sahara.

Being wordless, the act was truly international; I would imagine they played most theatres in the world and heaven only knows how many appearances at the London Palladium. In New York Ed Sullivan on television trawled the world for gold pieces like Wilson, Keppel and Betty to appear on his show.

For many young people who have never heard of them, I sympathise, but I don't apologise for including Wilson, Keppel and Betty among my Comedy Heroes.

ROB WILTON

The day war broke out

PROFILE

Born: (Robert Wilton Smith) 28 August 1881

Place of Birth: Liverpool

Rob trained as an engineer before starting out in the theatre in straight dramatic roles. While waiting in the wings to go on as a prison warder, he picked up a cap several sizes too small and the roars of laughter from the audience encouraged him to try his hand at comedy. In many of his famous sketches he was assisted by his wife, Florence Palmer.

Selected radio: *Mr Muddlecombe*

Selected flims: *The Secret of the Loch* (1934), *A Fire Has Been Arranged* (1935), *Stars on Parade* (1935), *It's Love Again* (1936), *Chips* (1938)

Died: 1 May 1957

I never saw Rob Wilton live on stage much to my sorrow, but I heard him many times on the wireless. Then, miraculously, one day I managed to catch him in one of his grainy black and white films. It had obviously been shot from the auditorium against a dark background with no audience.

It is sacrilege to ask one of the most outstanding funny men to perform in an empty hall merely for the archives. It's absurd, like drinking a vintage wine from a plastic cup. A singer or a juggler, even a contortionist (whatever that is) can perform without an audience, but definitely not a comedian – certainly not one as talented as Rob Wilton. The reaction of the audience is crucial to his act, which will change subtly every night according to his reception. The laughter he invokes provides his punctuation marks. They are his pauses while he creates more mirth by glancing in bewilderment round the hall, seemingly unable to grasp why they should be laughing.

This is the art of a good comedian, to orchestrate an audience, take them up with you and glide them gently into the next sally. In other words, I am cursing the fact that we do not possess a true assessment of Rob Wilton, although I am sure there is plenty of broadcasting material, it is just as important to be able to visualise the man at work.

He was a flustered, bumbling, portly, crumpled figure of a man. His expression was woeful, worried, as if he was carrying a burden too much for one person. Whenever he spoke it was with great deliberation in a pedantic, thoughtful rhythm as if each syllable was a masterpiece to be enjoyed. Should he be sitting behind a desk, his hand would be cupping his cheek as he nibbled the top of his little finger, and if he was standing, his left hand was cupping his right elbow for his usual sucking the little finger bit.

He addressed the audience as if every one of them was a long-lost friend he'd just met in the street and he spoke slowly and precisely as though he were giving advice to a slightly retarded child, a foreign one at that. He epitomised a harassed official surrounded by bewildered electors unable to grasp the clarity of his political gobbledegook.

For example, recounting to a delighted audience an exchange with his wife, he began with his ever popular introduction, 'The day war broke out . . .' Here he nibbled the top of his little finger, enabling him to marshal his thoughts. '. . . my wife said to me, "What are you going to do about it?" I said, "Who?" She said, "You!" I said, "Me?" She said, "Yes." I said, "Oh!" These lines from 'I said "Who?"' to the '"Oh!"' would be delivered in a rush like a scattering of loose stones under a mountaineer's boot.

Rob would carry on with his explanation. 'I'm in the LDV, aren't I?' he said.

'What's LDV, then?'

Exasperated, Rob said, 'Local Defence Volunteers.'

'Oh,' she said, 'Is it just you?'

'No, there's me, and Tom, and Fred from the garage, there's about twelve of us altogether.'

'Aye, and what do you reckon to be doing then?'

Now he gazed up to the ceiling, sighed and said, 'I said, "We're guarding the coast and when the Germans land I step forward and arrest Hitler." She looks at me after a while and says, "How will you know which one is Hitler?"'

And with the classic punch-line of all time, he ends the monologue by saying, 'I've got a tongue in my head, haven't I?'

The wording was priceless. Had it been 'I can ask somebody' or 'I've seen pictures of him', any other pay-off line would not have the same impact. 'I've got a tongue in my head, haven't I?' will be remembered as long as 'The day war broke out'.

In another film of his act, he was the fire brigade chief sitting at a table attending to whatever bureaucracy demanded when an excited young lady dashed on stage and said, breathlessly, 'Are you the Fire Brigade?' To which Rob replied, 'Not all of it, no.'

'Quickly!' she screamed. 'My house is on fire.'

Rob tried to calm her down. 'Don't get excited,' he spoke waveringly. 'With the best will in the world we can't set off until Arnold gets back with the fire engine.' And, apologetically, 'It's his turn to get the chips, you see.'

He then proceeded to take down her name and address, next of kin, etc. All the time he seemed impervious to her panic and as the young lady became more hysterical, he uttered inanities such as, 'Is it a big fire?' and enquired, 'Would it necessitate both hosepipes? With all the hot weather I've let the cricket club use one to keep the pitch moist.' Through all this the girl was pacing up and down in a panic. Rob, immune to her antics, carried on with his paperwork, in between platitudes such as, 'Is this your first fire?'

'Yes, yes,' she screamed.

'It may be your first fire but it's not ours.' He continued with his paperwork. 'What's your address?' he said.

'Clutterball Avenue,' she screamed. He looked at her amazed.

'I know it,' he said. 'It's just opposite the dry cleaners. What a stroke of luck. I've got a pair of trousers I can drop off there while we're at it.'

Finally the lady, in despair, dashes off stage while Rob

shouts after her, 'Just keep it going till we get there.'

These are just two examples of his humour. It is impossible to do him justice with these words and, sadly, we will never see his like again.

As a footnote, I would like to add that in the early 50s I was in a theatre bar in Birmingham. For a moment I thought I was alone but when I glanced round I saw a dejected old man at a brass-topped, round table, gazing into his half of beer. Then it hit me like a flash, it was Rob Wilton, one of my Heroes of Comedy. Apart from the lady behind the bar we were the only two customers. I desperately wanted to go up to him to thank him for all the pleasure he'd given me over the years. I wanted to buy him a drink. The lady behind the bar whispered, 'That's Rob Wilton.'

I nodded but I was too shy and too cowardly to approach him. I left taking with me a memory and a regret I bear to this day.

VICTORIA WOOD

Can't be bad to have a station named after you

PROFILE

Born: 19 May 1953

Place of Birth: Prestwick, Lancashire

Victoria gained a BA in Drama and Theatre Arts at the University of Birmingham and appeared on local radio and television before making a big impact nationally on the TV talent show *New Faces*.

Selected TV: *That's Life!* (1976), *Talent* (1979), *Nearly a Happy Ending* (1980), *Two Creatures Great and Small* (1981), *Wood and Walters* (1982), *Victoria Wood: As Seen on TV* (1984-86), *An Audience with Victoria Wood* (1988), *Victoria Wood* (1989), *Victoria Wood Live in Your Own Home* (1994)

Victoria and I have met socially on only one or two occasions. I've never eaten, played tennis, or danced with her but then I've never danced with Laurel and Hardy either and it doesn't exempt them from my list of Comedy Heroes. It certainly does not disbar Victoria Wood.

Perhaps referring to Victoria as a hero and not a heroine will bring the politically correct down on my head. I don't care; the last time I had down on my head I was six months old and I got over that.

I know little of Victoria Wood as a person, but then if I had to know all my icons personally before I included them in my hit parade, this would be a very thin book. Indeed, it would be more of a pamphlet.

It is not enough just to express my admiration for her and all the rest of my heroes, I should also explain why they have a place in my treasure house of memories. The answer is simple – they make me laugh. I am mesmerised by the economy of movement they employ to achieve this and, like Oliver Twist and his bowl, I want more.

Victoria Wood studied drama at Birmingham University. Now there is a turnaround. At least after she graduated she didn't take up doctoring; even if she had I've no doubt her patients would leave her surgery laughing so much they would forget what they came for in the first place. She has a great variety of talents – her writing, her acting, her musical wonders. She played the piano, accompanying herself with lyrics she had written, a small lonely figure in the vast confines of the Albert Hall, no less. You've got to have a degree in music before you can even busk outside there and, unless you're an orchestra or a ballet group from Russia, a booking at the Albert Hall will be as remote and unlikely as a government promise, but Victoria managed it. She had the audience in the palm of her hand, she was magnificent, it was a sell-out. I should know, I couldn't get a ticket. The great Noel Coward would have applauded with genuine appreciation. In fact, brilliant as he undoubtedly was, I cannot remember him ever appearing at the Albert Hall and if he did, please don't write in.

As a comedy writer she is amongst the elite, sitting at the top table. Years at a university cannot make you a writer, nor is it necessary to splash out on expensive equipment. To be a writer all that is required is a sheet of paper and a pencil, so it is to her eternal credit that, out of a population of sixty million people in this country, there are no more than a couple of handfuls of good writers and Victoria Wood is most definitely one of them.

Male writers sometimes find it difficult to write comedy lines for women. Victoria, however, has no problem writing for men and as for writing comedy for women, one only has to mention Julie Walters. It comes as no surprise to me that theatrical agents, and the BBC, had ignored these two talented people. Agents are not what they used to be, i.e. spotters of early budding talent, nursing and encouraging them until they are ready to be presented for public approval. Sadly, in this present mad rush through life, there is not the luxury or the time to groom new talent and the agents seem to have their sights set on those who are already successful. They have a living to make. The people at the BBC, however, do not really have this excuse; their livelihood is assured. But as Victoria was a pianist, singer and lyricist, with a leaning towards comedy, the BBC could not decide in which pigeonhole to put her. Victoria Wood and Julie Walters found each other. They became my two best-loved characters on television.

Their first show together, *Wood and Walters*, was

screened by Granada TV in 1980. On the success of this show the BBC discovered her and we were treated to the delightful series *Acorn Antiques*, followed by *Dinner Ladies* in which Thora Hird, Dora Bryan and myself made guest appearances. We didn't have much to do. Thora, bless her, in a wheelchair, Dora her garrulous self and me, played three elderly parents of three of the staff, a sort of parents' day. They were only small cameo roles but we would have agreed to appear had we only had one line. This was a credit to Victoria and the respect she engendered. Needless to say, we enjoyed the day immensely, reminiscing about the old days, the old jokes and old acquaintances, and the episode was, as always, brilliantly written.

For us, the highlight of the day came during our scene when we sat at a table eating real sandwiches and cake. Why was that such a treat? As explained in an old actor's reminiscences: 'The money isn't good but there's a practical steak and kidney pudding in the second act.'

Many hopefuls must be watching Victoria, fervently wishing they could be in her place if only they had the breaks. But it's useless sitting there bemoaning the unfairness of life when the question they should be asking themselves is would they be prepared to go through all the indignities of auditions? Which is what Victoria had to do – along with hundreds of others – queuing all night for an audition the following morning. Incidentally, one of these chancers was a sixteen-year-old Lenny Henry, all geared up to do Max Bygraves impressions. Back to our wannabes. In the unlikely event of walking out on stage to do an audition, is there anything you can do? Are you a juggler, a ventriloquist? Can you ride a unicycle or tear a telephone book in half? After one audition Victoria was told she had nothing to offer, that there was no place for her to work, and that she would never work. Those chilling words would have sent many a hopeful straight back to their old job. Instead, Victoria was determined to prove them wrong and, although she hardly worked for the next four years, she still came out of her corner fighting.

It is now ages since I've seen Victoria; 'Theatre' is the name of a small village in which every so often we all meet. But even if it is years since our last get-together, I know it will seem as though we met only yesterday. I've no doubt Victoria and I will come across each other soon, and she won't have changed from the girl I remember on the fringes of success: quiet, unassuming, with a faraway look in her eyes, apparently unseeing, but missing nothing.

A Children's Treasury of Milligan
Classic Stories and Poems by Spike Milligan

A Children's Treasury of Milligan is a delightful anthology
of stories and poems by the much-loved and sadly-missed
genius that is Spike Milligan.

Spike did not regard children as small adults, but as an
entirely different species who live in a secret, magical world
that very few adults understand. For decades he delved into
this world, delighting children – and adults – of all ages with
his poems and stories.

This book features some of Spike's classic children's work,
including *Silly Verse for Kids* (1959), *The Bald Twit Lion*
(1968), *A Book of Milliganimals* (1968), *Unspun Socks from
a Chicken's Laundry* (1968), *Sir Nobonk and the terrible,
awful, dreadful, nasty Dragon* (1982), and *Startling Verse for
All the Family* (1987).

Illustrated throughout with Spike's own drawings and
specially commissioned artworks, and featuring a CD of
Spike reading his poems aloud, this is an ideal book for
Spike fans of all ages.

The Eric Sykes Compendium

The Eric Sykes Compendium is a bumper edition of three novels from the comedy genius, including *Smelling of Roses*, *UFOs Are Coming Wednesday* and *The Great Crime of Grapplewick*.

- **Smelling of Roses** – Sparks and Miller are two ordinary soldiers desperate to avoid war who can hardly believe their bad luck when they hit the headlines as full-blown heroes.
- **The Great Crime of Grapplewick** – The sleepy northern town of Grapplewick is turned on its head when clueless criminals Terence and Rembrandt turn up seeking revenge.
- **UFOs are Coming Wednesday** – When a mysterious visitor demonstrates his amazing alien powers to the local dignitaries of Grapplewick, rumours fly and hysteria mounts.

With characters and situations that are pure Sykes, this volume is a bundle of laughs.

'Funny. Read it' Spike Milligan on *UFOs Are Coming Wednesday*

'...belly laughs that lurk in ambush behind every dune...'
Mail on Sunday on *Smelling of Roses*